The Kid Code

30 Second Parenting Strategies

Conscious (Less Stress) Parenting
2nd Edition

"I love your book. Your work is phenomenal. This is
a book that has so many useful techniques, strategies,
understandings, principles, it should be given to every
mother before they walk out of a hospital. People need
what you have. This is kind of an owners-manual
from God. It's beautiful. This is one of the best
parenting books I've ever read. Get this out there."
-Jack Canfield, **Bestselling Author**
Chicken Soup for the Soul Series

Brenda Miller, Bestselling Author

BALBOA.PRESS
A DIVISION OF HAY HOUSE

Balboa Press books may be ordered through booksellers or by contacting:

Balboa Press
A Division of Hay House
1663 Liberty Drive
Bloomington, IN 47403
www.balboapress.com
844-682-1282

Print information available on the last page.

ISBN: 978-1-9822-6950-0 (sc)
ISBN: 978-1-9822-6951-7 (e)

Balboa Press rev. date: 08/09/2021

Endorsements

"As a new parent, I have read many books and searched many sites on the internet looking for guidance and answers. The parenting principles presented by this course [The Kid Code] is really all I ever need and is beautiful in its simplicity."

Karlette Tunaley,
Mom and Yoga Teacher

"The strategies in The Kid Code took the anger out of parenting for me. They're super simple, and quick. I'm not saying this lightly - my whole parenting life changed. I now have this back-up support (The Kid Code) which gives me time in the moment to think – "Can I do this another way?" I find I catch myself just as I'm ready to bring out the 'undertaker voice', count to 3, order them to get to their room, or just yell at them because that seemed to work – but I had to ask myself, "Am I ruining my kids?" I knew I needed another way to parent and I found it in what I call the 'modern' techniques Brenda shared with me."

Chris Veltheim,
Founder, Course Rebel

"I am thankful for the path that took me to meet Brenda and thankful that she is such an amazing presence and present (!) in my life, helping me uncover my true self and giving me tools to navigate when I am not sure where to go."

Jackie S.

"Of the many gifts Brenda has given me over the years, one of the best is that she is able to show me a larger picture of what I am being shown in my life when I am unable to see. Brenda does this with such compassion, humility and kindness that it is impossible not to receive the message being offered. Along with this she has given me the tools to do much of this work myself."

Michele S.

"Brenda Miller's KID CODE is an incredible course assisting parents and children alike to experience challenges in an awakened, conscious state. The Kid Code challenges adults not only to increase effective parenting skills, but also the art of self-discovery and the ever-important aspect of "mirroring". Brenda's compassion and non-judgemental personality and coaching style makes KID CODE a nurturing, rewarding, and impactful course. Thank you, Brenda and Course Rebel for an amazing journey into waking up!"

Julie Veresh,
CBP- Innate Dynamics

"Kid Code was a very eye-opening parenting experience. Brenda is very knowledgeable and insightful and offers many techniques to apply to yourself and your kids. The tools are very useful and bring all kinds of awareness. This course will leave you feeling much more connected to your children, as well as forgiving, understanding, and easier on yourself as a parent. What a wonderful opportunity to experience The Kid Code. Thank you so much for sharing this incredible information! I am incredibly grateful!"

Kristin Pierce,
MindScape Instructor, AdvCBP

These techniques have already helped me to parent in a way that feels like I'm helping my children grow, and not dictating to them or endlessly arguing. The Kid Code offered me almost exactly what I was searching for. It provided me with a different outlook; ways that felt so much more effective and natural to me. It also provided me with different approaches to take in dealing with every day issues, with techniques that are very simple to use. I truly feel that Kid Code has ultimately helped me to parent so much better, and the information has helped me personally as well. Brenda is an incredible teacher, and, has new ways of helping you see life and the challenges you can face when parenting - in ways that help you find relief.

Janna Glasman

"This lady is a game changer."

Eric M.

"Over the years Brenda's compassion and wisdom have guided me through tough emotions and confusion - to calmness and clarity. This work has helped me feel less pain and more relief in my body. My daughter is grateful that I use these parenting strategies. They have provided a foundation that brings an ease to our communication and our relationship."

Louise Sevigny
Reiki Master, B.A. in Recreation Therapy,
Co-Owner of Your Good Company Ltd.

Other Books For Your & Your Child's Wellbeing

— *Blessing Mistakes* comes from one of the strategies in *The Kid Code* that teaches people how to give themselves and others Grace instead of grief when a mistake is made. There is magic in the message: "You matter more than the mistake." Learn more and join the movement: www.blessingmistakes.com

Coming Soon:

— *Mr. Upalupagus's Secret Secret's* is a compilation of fifteen children's bedtime or anytime stories (for the whole family) that reduce stress and uncover our natural state of joy. Mr. Upalupagus is a wise young elephant who takes his little-bit rowdy, but lovable crew on outer adventures around the world only to discover something beautiful about their inner selves using his secret secrets. It teaches kids the strategies in *The Kid Code*: www.mrupalupagus.com

— *BullyProof YourSelf (And Your Kids)* teaches parents, from a conscious perspective, how to end bullying. www.bullyproofyourselfandyourkids.com

To contact Brenda about becoming a Kid Code teacher: contact@thekidcode.ca

Contents

Acknowledgements

Thank you to my husband, kids and grandkids for their support and inspiration. Thank you to all children for showing us what our true nature is. Thank you to Jack Canfield, bestselling author of the Chicken Soup series for supporting this work with the certainty that it will help kids and their parents stop their suffering. Thank you to the early Kid Code teachers: Amanda Miller, Lasha Watson, Tyla Johnston, Louise Sevigny, Janna Glasman, Trista Davis, and Julie Veresh – and to all the teachers who come after you – for wanting to help parents reduce their stress, and kids stay in their nature! I am forever grateful to you for spreading this work and making the world a better place for all of us to live. Thank you to the many people who do this work and can testify to the peace it brings into their lives. Thank you to the superb publishing team at Balboa Press. Lastly, thank you to you for making your life and your child's life joyful – with these simple strategies.

Dedicated to my dad, who taught me
the joy of not judging others.

Preface

> "If you want to be happy, you have
> to go where happiness is."
>
> -Vernon Howard

This book, *The Kid Code*, is a wellbeing manual for parents, grandparents, coaches, educators, and, for all human beings who know a child. It's also for anyone who would like to feel joy and at ease in any situation.

It came about because I fell into the lap of many Masters who **live/d without stress**. That seems impossible, and yet, once I saw it was real for them, I began to wonder what the difference was between them and me. I wanted to know if it was possible for the rest of us to live that way: stress-free and happy. And, honestly, I didn't know where true, long-term happiness came from.

While I didn't believe living without stress could be achieved, over time, and after devouring the Master's teachings like a starving child, I began to understand that I had everything backwards because of my misunderstandings about the cause of, and the cure for, stress. What I learned from the Masters is that once we understand the true cause of stress, we can set ourselves free from it. When that happens, a natural and peaceful way to exist and parent becomes possible.

Ellen Galinsky of the Families and Work Institute asked 1,000 kids, "If you had one wish about your parents, what would it be?" **The kids said they wished their parents were less tired and stressed.** That's understandable, we don't like to be around stressed-out people either.

Kids used to say they wanted their parents to play with them and spend more time with them.

This book is about understanding the cause and the cure for stress; it's about making stress disappear!

The Masters I've studied and refer to often in this book are: Eckhart Tolle, Guy Finley, Byron Katie, Sadhguru, Mooji, Adyashanti, Vernon Howard, The Buddha, Jesus, Yoganada, The Dalai Lama, John De Ruiter, Osho, and others, including the work in *A Course In Miracles*. You can find detailed information about them at the end of the book. Other wise people I've studied the work of and included are Dr. Wayne Dyer, Louise Hay, Dr. Joe Dispenza, Joseph Campbell, Suzi Lula, Dr. Shefali Tsabary, and many more.

The Masters live from a natural and different perspective than most of us do: no person, event, or situation can affect their stress-free, peaceful state. They love everything and everyone with such genuine affection that it leaves one speechless, genuinely questioning what life is all about. They don't have conditions, expectations or demands on anyone or anything as a way to make themselves feel good. They don't *want* anything from anyone. It's natural for them to be joyful without a reason. It's natural for them to work towards the same state they live in for all human beings. It's natural for us, too, but we need some pointers to get back to our natural stress-free state of joy.

As parents, and, as human beings, we need answers. How can *we* live like they do?

As *A Course In Miracles* says, "Why would you seek an answer other than the answer that will answer everything?" This book has some of the answers we need as parents.

Who better to learn from than those who live without stress; those who live with a natural kind of happiness? Kids and Masters.

Children Teach us What They Want us to Teach Them

Children are not things to be molded,
but are people to be unfolded.

-Jess Lair

They may be four feet shorter than us, but kids are ten times wiser. They belly laugh, don't hold grudges, make friends easily, and don't register skin color, status, or body size. They are innocent, spontaneous, curious, and genuine. They don't know how to criticize and are naturally affectionate.

They want us to teach them THAT is who they really are.

They want us to teach them that they can draw on that part of themselves no matter what's going on in their lives.

Kids are not governed by 'things'; they don't care how important we are or what position we hold in our family, career, community, or country. They have never made a comment on the make of a car, the size of a house, or the clothes someone is wearing.

They *are* magnificent teachers.

It's okay to have a nice house and a car with a personal license plate, a career, and anything else that's in our lives; kids would like us to know that those things are not what really matter in life. We know that but are easily drawn into making unimportant things into important things.

When we do that, we cause ourselves a lot of stress.

Guy Finley, a prominent spiritual and self-help teacher, points out that what we own (the car, the house, etc.) begins to own us. We get ourselves a job: we have to make payments, maintain them, and worse, those things gain importance that they don't have.

We drift away from the natural state we see in children and fall into the trap of putting value and meaning on 'things' or 'ideas', like my child 'should do well' without knowing that 'do well' really means feeling at ease in their own skin, not winning a race, looking good, or getting 100% on a test.

Kids can play for hours with almost nothing (a stick, rocks, or a cardboard box) and be in their glory; that's because the glory is inside of them already. Their inner joy creates their experience of life. They aren't asking life (or anything or anyone in it) to make their experience what it is. They project their inner state of joy out onto anything that's in front of them. If that is true, then working on the inner state is the cure for outer problems (problems we experience with others, with situations, and with events).

All of that is what kids want us to teach them.

As Sadhguru, world renowned spiritual and wellbeing teacher, points out, if we were joyful when we were younger (and didn't register things like skin color and house size), shouldn't that have matured into something greater as we grew up? Where did all those wonderful ways of being in the world go as we got older? I wondered why we, as adults, lost those qualities and, instead, felt a lot of stress and pressure.

I could see the natural wisdom in a child, and realized it was because they hadn't yet been conditioned by beliefs about all of those things: skin color, status, body image, or wealth.

It struck me like a lightning bolt when I realized beliefs (in skin color, status, wealth, etc.) were at the root of all discord. The 'thing' itself wasn't stressful (body size, skin color, wealth – none of those are stressful) until we believe something about them.

If we don't have a belief about those things, there can be no opinion or prejudice that can gets us all stirred up about them. All of those things only took on importance when we (as parents, or as a society) believed they did, and then, either implied or insisted those opinions mattered and were true. We also taught our kids to let those ideas define who they are. We didn't teach those ideas knowing they would cause stress. We taught them hoping that it meant we had value, that we mattered, or that we would somehow be safe if we were 'better than' the other. We (mostly) unknowingly teach all beliefs.

Kids operate without the need for beliefs. So do the Masters.

It's natural for them to exist without believing anything. A child doesn't need to believe in anything to smile, reach for your hand, eat, walk, or talk. That's what we've forgotten: we can exist naturally without needing to believe.

When beliefs take over, stress is the outcome because beliefs, as Eckhart Tolle, an awakened spiritual teacher, says, are thoughts that can't validate themselves.

We think our lives have meaning because of our beliefs. The truth is that our lives have meaning because we are part of Creation. That's enough. We are enough as we are, without adding anything to ourselves (like a belief that separates and limits us). An example is that we all have the belief that we are better than someone else. Right now, think of the person you consider yourself to be better than. Is it a truth just because it's a belief? In reality, the belief that we are better than another is limiting and separating, not true.

Beliefs are not truths.

We veered away from our natural selves when we started agreeing with beliefs and not testing them for ourselves to see if they were true and if they served us.

Truth serves each and every human being - no exceptions.

If we observe kids, one of the first things they teach us is to be natural; pretending to be anything other than what we are, causes huge amounts of stress.

The last thing kids teach us is that they are an independent life: not better than, not less than; just human beings who arrived here a bit later than we did. They have a life to live.

In between kids will give us an education we never counted on, couldn't get from any place else, and, in the end, will be so grateful for.

As Rainer Rilke so beautifully put it: "There are two lives being lived." If you think of your child in this way, a lot of stress falls away. We don't have to control every aspect of our child's lives. We don't have to have an opinion on what they should do with their lives. They have a life and it's being lived - by them.

We, as parents are stewards to our children. What kind of steward depends on how many or how few ideas we have and if those ideas are in alignment with the way the world really works - or not.

Much of our stress comes from a belief that if we control the child, both our kids and we, will be acceptable and safe in the world. It's a belief, not a truth.

Trying to control another person, no matter what their age is - causes us a lot of stress. If we stop and think for a moment, we can see that we don't like being controlled, so it makes sense that others don't either (even kids). When we understand that guiding and protecting the child helps them grow, and, controlling them teaches them to feel anxious, we naturally fall into a different way of relating to them.

Kids blossom and shine without trying to. To blossom means to feel fresh, and alive, experience beauty everywhere, feel exuberant, and love what we're doing. It also means to develop natural talents, not to (only) point them towards a job, a family, and a mortgage.

The strategies in this book work because they are based in truth, and anything that is based in truth works. The truth breaks the barriers that keep us feeling like we're not enough and that we don't belong. It also ends the pointless obsession we have with wanting something or someone to please us, complete and fulfill us. The truth also washes away the hurts inside of us and leaves us joyfully at ease with life, even in challenging times.

The truth is a natural stress eliminator.

The result of this work is that it uncovers truth, and that uncovers love: plain and simple.

A Joyful Intervention!

"Miracles come in moments. Be ready and willing."
-Wayne Dyer

Before you go further, you are invited to read and apply the strategy called Blessing Mistakes.

It's been my experience that it can reduce stress in the household by 50% on day one of everyone learning it, experiencing the feeling it brings, and using it on all mistakes and negative states!

If you slow yourself down when a mistake is made or when a negative state arises, and you use this simple strategy, (or any other strategy in *The Kid Code*) you're giving yourself an intervention that is *for your wellbeing.*

Dr. Joe Dispenza, who spent his post graduate studies in neuroscience and brain function has proof that when we get upset with negative emotions, our brains create negative chemicals which the body and mind will use for negative thinking and negative actions. In other words, negativity is biologically addictive and becomes habitual. https://drjoedispenza.com

That's not good for our wellbeing.

Bringing ourselves into a calm and coherent state instead of giving in to big emotional upheavals or becoming negative, saves more than relationships – it saves our bodies too.

Kids Naturally Shine

All blossoms captivate us.

Each of us wants our kids to be joyful inside, not only during their childhood, but also as adults. We'd love the same for ourselves but don't seem to have the formula for that.

While we don't usually think of ourselves as able to shine, that's what's waiting inside of each of us. If we peel away the layers of beliefs that cause us stress, one by one, we won't have any other choice than to shine. Shining happens when our True Self operates us as opposed to beliefs operating us.

How we know that is true is because when we are in states of gratitude, compassion, generosity, joy, peace, and authenticity, inside of us, we don't feel as though anything is wrong. We *feel* natural. It's our True Nature, our True Essence, our True Inner Self. When we are in states of anger, worry, sadness, grief, fear, or distress of any kind, we, *don't feel natural*. Those states don't feel natural to us because *they aren't* natural to us. They are the indicator that we are out of alignment with the truth.

As we uncover natural joy in ourselves, we can teach our kids, first by modelling the ways to naturally feel lit up, and next, by making the ways that do that for us a daily part of our conversations with them.

When we model what's important and talk about what's important, our kids grow up knowing what's important.

Our inner state is the most important thing in our own lives. If *it's* shining, then we project that out onto our children, onto what we do, what we say, and that state governs how we treat others.

It's not a dream to be able to shine on the inside while there's chaos on the outside; it's our main purpose as human beings. We are most genuinely and joyfully useful to ourselves, others, and to the planet in that state of being.

If our purpose is shining on the inside and on the outside, and I can't think of a better one, and others have achieved that state, then a pathway must be here for us to follow, and it is.

Sustainable Moments

Making sure you get what you need,
ensures you give what you can.

There is rightfully a lot of common-sense talk around the globe about the importance of sustainability, which means to get needs met without depleting or compromising resources for the future.

The best way to sustain our families, our homes, our communities, and our world, is to first sustain ourselves.

What sustains human beings, besides the essentials that sustain life itself: food, water, air, sunlight, movement, etc.? If you could make a list of other things that sustain you, bring you aliveness and inner joy, what would be on that list? Some examples are: being in nature, spiritual practices, playing, etc.

Sustain yourself daily - until you fall into Grace and that sustains you.

Being Drawn into the Chaos isn't a Requirement

You can learn many things from children.
How much patience you have, for instance.
-Franklin P. Jones

We teach what we know, and beliefs are what we know.

Answer this simple question.

Where did you learn your beliefs from?

Parents, school, culture, etc.

'Learn' is the key word.

Beliefs are learned and can be unlearned. They are not part of our nature.

Beliefs cause and draw us into chaos.

An example is, if we believe we're right about something and we have an upset feeling along with it, a learned belief has been challenged. When we're right without a belief, there is a solid knowing without the urge to argue, defend or fight about it.

It is inevitable that kids are going to obscure some, or a lot of their Natural Selves or True Nature, and unknowingly rely on what causes stress: beliefs, ideas, opinions, prejudices, and thoughts. Those are the very things that will also help them come back, full circle, to their Natural Selves, if they are taught how to use upsets to their advantage.

As we do more and more of the type of work that's in *The Kid Code*, we will begin to teach our children truths, not beliefs, and that will reduce the mental, emotional, and physical stress that beliefs cause, and at the same time, teach them how to handle upsets.

They don't have to live with stressful beliefs; neither do we. The Nature we all experienced as children is waiting there for us to uncover. It's not magic, it's not fanciful, it's the biggest and most beautiful part of every human being. We get glimpses of it now and then, but that's not good enough. Who doesn't want to live peacefully, feel natural no matter what we're doing, and laugh out loud, a lot?

With the strategies in this book, anyone can become the masters of their own lives and teach others how to do the same. Learning how to turn an upset into peace may be the most important thing we ever learn as human beings.

Life with Kids

Before I got married, I had six theories
about bringing up children.
now I have six children and no theories.
-John Wilmot, Earl of Rochester

When kids come into our lives, we feel emotions we never thought possible. Some of them hold us in pure, heart-opening awe; others, well...that's the reason for this book.

Kids give us experiences we'd never have without them. They make us laugh like we've never laughed before, make us cry like we never want to again, and push every single button we have. As parents, we would give anything to be calm while they're doing it!

Love them as we do, they lie to our faces, wipe their noses on our shirts, tell the teacher about the size of our bellies, recite little white lies that we tell them (as though they are absolute truths), and mischievously repeat all curse words we let slip.

It's a guarantee that they will whine, fuss, cry, scream, hit, bite, argue, and rebel. Sometimes, it seems inescapable that we have no choice but to get upset when they do. There is a way to stay calm/calmer while all that's going on; and it comes naturally to all of us. We've just lost touch with that part of ourselves that knows calmness IS the natural response. We've lost touch with that part of ourselves that knows how to respond instead of reacting.

Until we get there (to calmness) we are often inclined towards upset when our kids are hollering, hitting, or otherwise acting out. Sometimes it feels like the only response is frustration when they take up most of our time, three-quarters of the bed, and every spec of patience we have. We're lost when they won't eat anything green, create chaos in the house, and refuse to get dressed so everyone can get out the door on time. Still, with all of the upsets, when they smile, cuddle, and talk with us, everything feels right in the world.

Once, during a family crisis, my dad said, "You have fifteen minutes to be upset...if you want. And then you need to get calm for the sake of your kids and yourself." That simple teaching has stayed with me; I'm no good to myself or the other if I'm in chaos. We can be of the most help to ourselves and others if we are in a calm state.

If it's possible to stay calm on the inside while there is chaos on the outside like the Masters' do, and I can't think of a better way to live, then it would be to our advantage to follow their lead.

The Pathway to Peace

If everyone demanded peace
instead of another television set,
then there'd be peace.

- John Lennon

The pathway is not new. The secrets for true peace have been passed down since ancient times from wise men and women who arrived on the shores of peace long ago. In those days they chose a few people to teach the secrets to. Nowadays, pointers to the wisdom that pre-exists inside of us are everywhere, waiting for us to tap into them and free ourselves from stressful lives. All wisdom, eastern and western, says the same thing: peace can only be found inside of us.

We were never taught how to access it.

The simple 30 Second Parenting Strategies in this book are all about how to take the anger and confusion out of parenting and come back to love as a natural response - no pretending. And, no (or less) threatening, punishing, repeating ourselves, and mumbling nasty stuff under our breath, or worse, hollering it out loud.

When used long-term, long-term love and patience show up, and short-term craziness vanishes; or at least makes fewer, less-convincing appearances!

We were never taught how to deal with our own overwhelming emotional upsets and hair-raising behaviors, never mind what to do with our children's.

When using these strategies, you'll find that they give both you and your kids relief – in the moments of upset, or in the moments right after, and that's what we'd give anything for, as parents. It feels like a miracle when an upset dies a quick death leaving us feeling calm and peaceful.

Once Upon A Time

Remember the "Once upon a time" story?
Hahaha.

A child was born to parents who had dreams of teddy bears and lullabies, of first steps, and first words...of 'happily ever after'. Then they began to notice that, even though they were in charge of the child's wellbeing, they didn't really know what to do with temper tantrums or any of the other challenges that come with children, like what to do when they lie, refuse to do homework, or fight about chores. The 'happily ever after' was more like, "Oh, no, what happened to my life, who is this child, and what now? How does this little person with a limited vocabulary, and a supposedly undeveloped brain run my life?"

When they are two feet tall, we learn how terrifying the number two can be. We hope that something will change, and the perfectly behaved little human being we wish we had might appear.

How did they grow up and go from diapers and toothless grins, to baggy jeans and (color-coordinated) braces, and how did we go from us telling them bedtime stories to them telling us tall tales?

About the time we have a child, we believe we are sort of in control of our lives. Then along comes a child, and control slips out of our hands. It leaves us puzzled, frustrated and desperate for something to change - with no tools to create change. Worst of all, we secretly wonder if we are ruining or damaging our children.

Kids don't come with an instruction manual. They are one. It's written in code inside of their hearts and on their faces, and eventually in the words they speak and the actions they take.

Our children have the same purpose on earth as we do: to come into consciousness and live from that clear, connected place. The cultural prescription for a happy, successful life hasn't turned out a lot of happy, successful people. It's time for change. This book is 'how-to'.

Our kids, with their antics, will catalyze us into waking up if we use upsets wisely and that results in living from our natural, stress-free state.

'Waking up' means coming into a state of natural joy instead of staying 'asleep' and hanging on to beliefs that cause us pain. Being 'asleep' means we are unconscious, unaware, and always convinced we are right – and still stressed out.

If we're right, why are we so stressed out?

All we have to do, to begin, is to get honest. That means it's time to, without judging ourselves, recognize that the way we do things in the world doesn't work, even though we keep doing them and teaching them to our kids. It's important to begin by realizing that the way we're living isn't causing long-term, belly-laughing happiness.

With this work, we can have that happy ending that we were hoping for when we got married, had kids, got that job... Although, it's not really a happily-ever-after ending, it's more like a 'joyful being right now'. We can go to sleep at night feeling at peace with our day and wake up with appreciation for being alive. The 'Once Upon A Time' dream lies just ahead, but first, let's see what's gotten in the way of that.

The ABC's Of Life

Until we learn what matters,
we love what doesn't.

This book is really a simple kind of parenting 'school' where you don't memorize anything, don't have any tests, read for five minutes a day, and learn some stuff that will help you to feel comfortable in your own life.

It's good to know that one plus one equals two, BUT, it's vital to know how the world really works. It won't help us to think we know something if it isn't true. It isn't true that we are better than or worse than another human being. Yet, we go on thinking in those ways and acting from that beliefs like that.

Truth won't help us until we bring it into our understanding and experience.

For example, it's the truth that helping others (no matter who they are) is good. That won't really help us until we bring it into our experience. Once we experience it, it changes us because our understanding grows deeper: helping the other is the same as helping ourselves because it ignites love and connection inside of us.

The real ABC's of life are about how to:

Autentically Be Conscious.

A = Authentically (be respectfully curious about who we are and what we're doing here because we don't really know).

B = Be (focus on the Being part of us while respecting the human part).

C = Conscious (means being aware of the truth that serves everyone all of the time).

In that state, everyone's and everything's wellbeing IS the only concern.

Growing Up to Be Childlike

The child must know that he is a miracle, that since
the beginning of the world there hasn't been,
and until the end of the world there will not be,
another child like him.

-Pablo Casals

A lot of growing happens from ages zero to twenty, but not much growing up happens.

Adulthood IS for growing ourselves up. Unless we have reached our natural state of unlimited wisdom and harmlessness, we've got some gentle growing up to do!

This book won't just help you come back to sanity with regards to parenting, but it will help you grow all the way up to being joyfully childlike with the *benefit of* unlimited and pure intelligence: belly laughing, extending compassion to your fellow human beings, genuinely caring about everyone (and the earth), being joyful about waking up in the morning, and feeling grateful instead of grumpy. This is what happens when we grow up.

Once you do this work, you unlock the code that will blossom you and your child.

I want to share that with you. It is my greatest wish that when you read this book and apply the strategies that you experience peace immediately, that you teach your children how to do the same, and that this message, that many of us are working with, spreads across the planet and makes this a world we all want to live in.

Why Do Our Own Inner Work (Use these techniques on ourselves before we teach them to our children)?

My kid is turning out just like me.
Well played, karma. Well-played.

-Unknown

Love is what will happen to us if we do this work. Love, as our guide, feels better than ideas, beliefs, prejudices, and opinions as our guide.

There is another reason to do our own inner work asap:

"The past excretes into the future." Sadhguru

History repeats itself. Upsets and troubles keep repeating. If we want real change to happen, we have to look at ourselves and see what is inside of us that attracts the lives we have. What's inside of us that makes us react so negatively when we wish we wouldn't? The awareness we gain from doing this work is enough to change our future. If we want what's best for our children, we have to see what that means. This work shows us what's best for us and our kids.

If we uncover our True Nature, we uncover the treasure within us.

Our own inner pre-existing True Nature *is* the treasure. We can't share treasure until we find it. We can't teach another to find theirs until we find our own. We can't assure another that the treasure we seek is right here inside of us until we find it here ourselves.

Who Can Use This Book?

Children are the living messages
we send to a time we will not see.
                                                      -John F. Kennedy

Anyone who knows a child and wants their future to be truly bright.

Anyone who wants to feel aliveness, secure, compassionate, loving, grateful, genuine, and playful.

Anyone who wants to discover truth.

Anyone who wants to become creative.

Any parent, grandparent, educator, coach, or caretaker can use the techniques on themselves and then teach them to children. When we do, children, no matter the age, begin to naturally come into conscious living. Why does that matter? Because conscious living has less stress, and kids need less stress to make a peaceful future.

You don't have to be a parent to use the strategies in this book, you just need to want to feel better inside - no matter what's going on in your world.

The choice is to be a loving steward to ourselves and our kids, or to be unconscious and in mental and emotional pain.

The unsuccessful ideas we collected for successful living come back again and again because we weren't aware of the cause of them. We're very aware of the pain they bring. Anything that brings pain is meant to be questioned.

After age seven, you can begin to teach children the ideas found in this book. Your children will benefit if you do the work on yourself before they reach the age of seven because you will be a calm parent modelling conscious and calm living. Some children will need to be a bit older to grasp some of the concepts. You will intuitively know when and which strategy to teach them. Be prepared to be amazed when your children respond to them even more quickly than you!

Guy Finley suggests that when your children are under the age of seven, the best you can do for them is your own self-inquiry work based on what you are seeing in them that you don't like.

I love Sadhguru's advice: leave young kids alone, let them play and don't try to 'teach' them anything. They are born will pure intelligence and will pick up more if we leave them alone. That advice flies in the face of how we operate, and yet, he lives without stress, so I think trying it his way might be a good idea (at least some of the time).

Kids are 'monkey see, monkey do', that's why doing your work is so valuable to them. If you have a three-year-old and a six-year-old, you know what I mean. The younger one copies the older one exactly. As Sadhguru teaches, kids are observing us, not listening to us.

Even if you don't have children yet, you can use this book to help yourself become clearer before you do have kids, and then by the time they arrive, the strategies will be automatic.

Notice how our 'heads' have unsuccessfully taken over our hearts when it comes to teaching ourselves and our children.

You can't 'reason' with a very young child; the reasoning capabilities aren't developed enough – yet we go on trying. In that way, we are the irrational ones if we think we can reason with someone incapable of it. In that case, doing our own work is essential so we can at least keep ourselves calm and sane, while others aren't.

If you have older children who are not yet open to this kind of work, doing this work will change how you feel about them – and that's enough. We don't know what every person needs to experience to help them along the way. Once we know how this work makes us feel inside, we'll want to share it with our kids and that's great. Share it, but if they resist, let them. You make yourself happy – they'll want to follow.

When kids (or others) are 'losing it', it's nice to be calm, which is what this work does – that means anyone can use this book to keep from 'losing it', and to be unaffected or less affected by people who are.

When I'm the caretaker of any child, we use one of the strategies in this book to change the upset feelings to peaceful feelings, and, then we can get right back to playing!

When I'm having a tantrum (even if I'm trying to hide it), I also use the techniques in this book on myself. It's instant relief for me and for those around me because I don't dump my nonsense onto them.

Anyone who gets sidetracked by a negative state can use the strategies found here. I still use them every day. Life is too short to be anything less than joyfully alive.

When to Use This Book?

If you could get out of mental or emotional
pain in a heartbeat, would you?

Whenever you feel an upset, use one of the strategies you like – that will take you out of it.

An upset is any time **you** feel any of these ways (no matter who is present or what is happening):

— Negative in any way. Some examples are: angry, confused, impatient, frustrated, cold-hearted, worried, scared, sad, hopeless, etc.
— Like there is a problem (big or small).
— Discomfort with thoughts, emotions, or actions.
— A contraction or tensing in the mind or body (other than with exercise).
— Uncomfortable in your own skin.
— When you are feeling 'off', or 'out of sorts'.
— Ego oriented (centered on the self – me, mine, my, self-importance). Being ego oriented is the opposite of feeling natural, so any time you don't feel natural, you can use one of the strategies.
— Falsely positive states: pretending to be happy, smiling when you don't mean or feel the smile inside of yourself, agreeing with someone when you just wish they'd be nicer/kinder, etc.

All upsets are coming from inside. They are the result of a belief acting out.

How to Use This Book?

You can't teach what you don't know.

There are several ways to use the strategies in the book effectively:

1. Read the information prior to the strategies and then read one strategy once a week, practicing it during upsets several times a day for the whole week.
2. Read it cover to cover (contemplating what's been said), and then go back and learn the strategies you are drawn to.
3. Or, any way you want to. Flip to a page and read it. Ponder the information and do the exercises.

It is necessary to learn and use the strategies until you experience relief with them yourself before you teach them to your kids.

By using the strategies, you will have masterminded your own 'peace' intervention and, most importantly, you will change how you feel inside when an upset arises because you know what to do with it. With time, you will notice you feel freer, more peaceful, and more joyful. The unexpected bonus is that something wonderful will come through you from Divine Intelligence that will make you shine on the inside and the outside.

This work makes space for Grace/peace.

How to Get the Most Out of Each Strategy?

We must learn to live together as brothers
or perish together as fools.
                    - Martin Luther King, Jr

Once you experience relief with the exercises, you will be able to share them with anyone and if they are interested, invite them to try it. Share it as though you have a secret that is like magic – you do, and it is!

Join our Facebook page 'Conscious Parents, Conscious Kids' (notice the comma) to ask questions about the strategies, about parenting, or just to share your experience of using the strategies.

30 Second Parenting Strategy
Blessing Mistakes

All people who make mistakes,
big or small, deserve love.
Karma takes care of their consequences.
Your kindness takes care of yours.

Learning how to give yourself and others Grace, not grief when a mistake is made is for everyone's wellbeing. With a clear understanding of Blessing Mistakes, it can reduce the stress in a household by 50% on the first day of using it!

Use this with your kids, partners, friends, family, co-workers; use it with anyone and everyone – even with yourself.

This stress-reducing, connection-creating strategy will change how you feel inside of yourself, how you feel towards others, and how others feel towards you. It puts the focus on the human being, not their mistake and it points us back to our True Nature.

It's natural to support someone when a mistake is made. How we know this to be true, is to see how we feel inside of ourselves when we offer true support.

Whatever feels natural *is* natural.

It doesn't feel natural to belittle, humiliate, shame, or devalue someone when they make a mistake. How we know this to be true is that if we check inside ourselves while behaving in those ways, we don't feel good or natural.

How To Bless a Mistake:

1. Someone else makes a mistake.

The mistake is already made, so now you can decide how you want to be and feel and act towards the person who made the mistake. Do you want to give them grief or give them Grace?

- If you give them grief, notice how awful you feel while you do it and how awful you feel long after you've done it (the misery keeps coming back and we keep thinking and talking to ourselves about it).
- If you give them Grace, notice how good you feel while you do it (it's a warm, compassionate, non-judgmental feeling). Giving the other Grace means showing kindness towards them.

It doesn't hurt to remember that we all still make many mistakes every day. That will help us want to give others Grace.

You say to them and feel the truth of the statement: "You matter more than the mistake." Use whatever language you feel conveys that the mistake doesn't de-value the person making it. Examples of what to say are:

- "Everyone makes mistakes. Lots of them."
- "Mistakes can be helpful!"
- "Mistakes are not meant to make us feel bad."
- "This mistake doesn't matter, you do."
- "Making mistakes is inevitable.'"
- "I feel good when I Bless my mistake and then make it right."
- "Some mistakes are meant to be a lesson to help us along the way."
- "Sometimes I get it wrong many times before I get it right."

2. **Part two of Blessing Mistakes: Make It Right, Learn From It, Let It Go.**

Make it right:

That means apologize, replace something, clean up something, or whatever will make it right. Why?

— Making it right feels good inside (check inside yourself to see).
— Each of us is 100% responsible for whatever we say or do. We think everyone else is responsible for what they say and do, so by that logic, we are also responsible for everything we say and do. Denial of a mistake or justifying a mistake feels bad inside of us. We don't want to make ourselves feel bad – we're aiming for our own wellbeing, not misery.

Learn from it:

— See if there is a lesson that can help you. "What did I learn that I'd like to change?"
— Maybe there is nothing to learn.

Let it go:

Once you've made the mistake right and/or learned from it, there is nothing else to do but to let it go – leave it in the past where is it.

Let it go means:

— Feel the uncomfortable feelings that arise around the mistake until they disappear.
— Invite yourself to 'burn it up' (as taught by Guy Finley). That means think about the mistake and ask for it to be burned

up, burned out of your consciousness. Feel what you feel until there is a release.

— Offer it to the Universe to transform.

— Surrender to the feeling of the mistake and let it naturally dissolve (once we are no longer arrogant and deny a mistake, it's easy to surrender to it).

3. You make a mistake.

— Bless yourself by saying to yourself, and feeling the truth of the statement, "I matter so much more than this mistake."

— Make the mistake right as best as you can, learn from it or leave it in the past, whichever is appropriate.

4. Someone makes a mistake, and you give them grief.

— Bless yourself for making the mistake of giving them grief and make it right with them. This is for your own wellbeing (and theirs).

5. You are negative.

— Being negative is not part of your nature, so it's a mistake. As soon as you notice you are thinking, feeling, speaking, or acting in a negative way, stop yourself, say and feel the truth of the statement, "I matter so much more than this mistake of being negative."

6. The other person is negative.

— As soon as you notice another person has a negative expression on their face, or is speaking or acting in a negative way, silently say and feel the truth of the statement, "You matter so much more than the mistake of being negative."

The 'Mistake Footprint'

When we don't bless a mistake, we leave a 'mistake footprint' inside of ourselves. That means we leave discomfort inside of ourselves that will rise up another day in another painful way.

It's healthier to resolve a mistake in the moment it's made.

Please teach this to anyone who is interested -
to reduce stress levels around mistakes.
We're making it a movement!!

Why Being Negative Is A Mistake

You didn't form your ego.
Your learned it.
Then it formed you.
Now it's your (negative) operating system.

Negativity is not normal. It's negative.

Negativity is not natural. It's unnatural. All we have to do to prove that to ourselves is to notice how we feel when we're negative.

Negativity comes from an identified part of ourselves, a conditioned, learned idea of who we are – it comes from our ego.

Our ego-identified personality thinks it's gaining something by being negative, and therefore keeps it at the ready as a (poor) strategy for life.

Examples of what we believe we are gaining by being negative:

— Being right.
— Being the authority.
— Being smarter than the other person.
— Being better than the other person.
— Getting me what I want.

The ego is the opposite of our Essential Nature, which is never negative, it has no need to be negative. That's why it's a mistake when we're ego-identified (and then become ego-operated).

When we're negative, we can reset ourselves by Blessing the mistake. It's a way to self-regulate and lift ourselves out of negativity.

When the other is negative, we can Bless the mistake instead of entangling in the negativity and making the situation worse.

How *Not* to Use Blessing Mistakes

Don't Use It to Avoid Responsibility

— If you make a mistake and bless yourself, and then don't make the mistake right, you are not giving yourself the relief that Blessing Mistakes can give you. It can't be used to avoid responsibility. As a reminder, if someone else makes a mistake who is responsible? They are of course. By that simple logic, if we make a mistake, we are responsible. Bless yourself for not taking responsibility and then take responsibility.

  o Notice how you feel inside when you take responsibility vs. making excuses, justifying, or denying a mistake.

Don't Use It (Out Loud) When the Other Doesn't Think They Made A Mistake

— You can't say, "Bless you" out loud to someone who doesn't think they've made a mistake, that will just make them mad and more defensive. You can silently say and feel "Bless you," to them – that's for your own wellbeing and to help you not get entangled in a negative situation.

Don't Use It with Strangers

— Unless you feel it's the right thing to do.
— They may not think they made a mistake and won't receive it well.
— They may think you are overstepping your bounds, and you are, if ego is involved.
— They won't know what you're talking about if you say, "Bless you," to them. They'll just think you're crazy and they'd be right if your ego thinks it needs to Bless anyone for anything. No one needs our blessing. The paradox is that when we genuinely bless someone they resonate with their own True Nature. When we give it to someone silently, that's for our own wellbeing.

It's normal to make mistakes.
It's not normal to have so much stress over them.

30 Second Parenting Strategy
The Tantrum Tamer

You can't put a lid on lava!

Use this when your child is having a tantrum (or you are).

1. My favorite, while someone is having a tantrum is to do Kegels or for the dads, recite baseball stats. In the midst of a volcano exploding, you can't put a lid on lava, so to keep yourself from exploding in reaction to a tantrum, it's good to distract yourself and do something useful. The one having the tantrum has to get over it sooner or later, and the more you engage, the more they will tantrum, unless....

2. When they can hear you over their own bellows, you can divert your energy into calmness and tell them, "It's so understandable that you feel that way," a statement taught by self-care expert, and author of *The Motherhood Evolution*, Suzi Lula (www.suzilula.com). I love this method and use it often. To have compassion for the other (while they are identified with wanting or some other painful attachment) is simply more humane. The one having the tantrum thinks they have a good reason for their tantrum. Until we/they can work out what the real problem is, compassion can sometimes be enough to reach them.

3. Keep yourself from touching them – when you're having a tantrum, you don't want to be touched (unless you do). Neither does a kid. (If your child is the exception, and you know your child responds to cuddling when a tantrum arises, then cuddle them). There is a

lot of energy being expressed. Let it blow. Then take action that won't further upset them.

4. When they are ready, offer them comfort. Don't punish them; you will hurt inside if you do. After a tantrum, when all is calm, see if you can find out what the real issue was. See if there is a real need for the child and help them meet it. They may feel something is unfair, so their need is to feel as though they matter. Tell them why they matter, and, that you try to make things right for everyone as much as possible and that everything doesn't always seem fair.

They may want the temporary high that a toy or candy will bring them. Help them feel good inside by making faces with them, giving them an important job, etc. Plan ahead when going out to increase the child's comfort and reduce their 'need' for a tantrum.

Some ideas for reducing temper tantrums in a store:

1. Remind them before you go into the store that you are not buying toys or candy today.
2. Take your own snacks and drinks into the store (when permitted).
3. Take a book for them to read.
4. Take comforting stuffies or favorite toys.
5. Make up stories about the farmer milking the cow to get the milk as you arrive at the milk cooler, and let your child give the farmer and the cow names; ask them to help with the stories.
6. Let them help get the groceries.
7. Engage them with a game: see if they can spot a letter of the alphabet or a picture on the cans and boxes, etc.

When I have an adult temper tantrum, I notice that the 'I-ness in my Highness' wants what she wants and there is no room for anything else. If she doesn't get it (such as respect, to choose the vacation spot, to merge onto a freeway without changing her speed, another hour of sleep, - it's a long list of demands - you know what I'm talking about) there is a temper tantrum. It's either expressed in the moment, or, suppressed to blow inwards or outwards at a later date.

As you do more and more work on your own upsets (tantrums) you will be able to be calmer when your child has one.

When you feel your own lava rising, you can:

Notice yourself working up to a temper tantrum and begin to watch the temper tantrum and not act it out or suppress it, but feel it fully until it dissipates. Don't focus on the other person involved, if there is one, just notice what's coming up inside of you and feel all the feelings until they disappear, as they are guaranteed to. This method takes a very conscious human being so don't be disappointed if you can't do it right away. We are all a WIP. If you can do this, you will notice that it ends the upset and the story, and the ranting in your head disappears. This method is powerful and peaceful.

My favorite is from Louise Hay who was a greatly admired spiritual self-help teacher and founder of Hay House, one of the world's largest promoters of human transformation.

> *"To me, habitual anger is like sitting in a corner with a dunce cap on."*
> *-Louise Hay*

That's an image that has impact.

Next time you begin to feel anger imagine yourself steaming away in a corner with a dunce cap on! The anger might even give way to laughter!

'Divert to Divinity.' Use one of the many strategies listed in that chapter to bring yourself back to a calm, coherent state.

'Take a moment' (as taught by Suzi Lula). Then take any action that doesn't hurt you or another person. For example, you could remove yourself from the room and let the anger express into a pillow. Although, it's necessary if you have an outburst, that you explain to others, if they see or hear you, that they are not the cause of the anger. We are the cause of our own anger by believing a pre-conditioned thought. Try this once; you'll be glad you did because you won't make matters worse by lashing out at someone. Eventually you will be able to graduate to being able to watch the tantrum without believing you need to act it out. That's what ends the tantrum's power and gives you your own peaceful power back.

John de Ruiter, a Canadian spiritual teacher shares a wonderful strategy for immediately dissipating frustration, anger, or rage (adult temper tantrums): write a note that says, "I don't need my raging story anymore," put it in your pocket and pull it out and read it every time you feel anything from slight irritation to full on rage. Then turn your attention to inside of yourself until your feel the natural peace that resides there.

If you act out a temper tantrum, the consequences will hurt you and others. It's good to remember this and see if you can take some deep breaths, remove yourself if necessary, and try to get some clarity.

30 Second Parenting Strategy
Dealing with Big Emotions

I often worry about the safety of my children especially the one that rolls their eyes at me and talks back.
                                        -A humorous parent.

Eckhart Tolle teaches that when a big emotion arises inside of us, it confuses us and then the words or actions that follow will be irrational.

Next time you have a big emotion (anger, fear, etc.), stop and notice that this process is actually taking place:

— the emotions are rising up inside of us,
— we start to feel confused; we are definitely not clear,
— and then our thoughts, words and actions become irrational.

When the emotion overtakes you (fear, worry, disgust, anger, sadness, grief, frustration, hopelessness, etc.), ask yourself, "Do I want to be confused and then irrational?" That's usually enough to discharge the energy and bring you back to balance and sanity.

Because this book is about wellbeing, for everyone in your house, notice that having big emotions doesn't feel like wellbeing (because it's not). It can be helpful to keep remembering what we discussed earlier: emotions cause mental and physical damage, are addictive and cause troubles in relationships. We don't need that in our lives anymore.

Teach this to your children. It can dissipate big emotions in seconds.

30 Second Parenting Strategy
Screen Time

One day I'll be thankful that my kid is strong-willed.
But that will not be today.
                                        -Another funny parent.

When the kids get home, or if they aren't in school yet, put all phones and gadgets in a box, as recommended by many experts, and designate a specific time for them. Other than during that time, they don't come out of the box. Most phones have a feature that allows parents to set a time limit.

Look at the time the child spends looking at a screen in relation to all other aspects of life:

> Play with others/siblings
> Homework
> Quiet and free play by themselves
> Chores
> School
> Family time

Personal care – caring for their physical person (bathing, showering, brushing hair and teeth, preparing, and eating nourishing meals, etc.).

Sleep

Self-care & Hobbies– doing things that fulfill them, nourish them, light them up, etc. Some examples are: crafts like drawing, painting and making robots. Other examples (for adults) are: photography, writing, walking in nature, gardening, yoga, meditation, daily gratitude practice, reading, listening to music that is connecting and uplifting, doing spiritual practices like self-inquiry, etc.

Find a balance between all aspects of daily life so life doesn't use its considerable forces to have you notice you're out of balance.

30 Second Parenting Strategies
Diverting to Divinity - Coherence & Connection

Having one child makes you a parent;
having two, you are a referee.

-*David Frost*

The strategies here bring us into coherence and connect us to a higher level of consciousness. The natural consequence of that is the feeling of deep peace, freedom, stillness, etc. They can also be considered automatic stress-reducers, because they bring our brain back into balance.

One way to use these pointers to your peaceful Inner Nature is to practice them as often as you can during the day when you are calm.

This strategy also makes space for Grace (peace).

The other way to use them is when you feel yourself going into an upset, ask yourself, "Do I want to go down this old pain-filled road that isn't really me and isn't really truth?" For me, the answer is always, "No." Then, use one of these many pointers to your True Nature.

Each of these pointers to peace must be felt experientially; in other words, practice it until you feel calmness, peace, joy, neutrality, gratitude, abundance – no pretending. Just stay with the exercise until you feel a shift. This state is also known as Isness, Beingness, Divine Intelligence, at one with Source, or Universal Intelligence. Grace, etc.

Words don't answer any of the questions below. There must be an 'experience of' the strategy to feel it's effect. If a word arises rather than an 'experience of', then sit quietly and repeat the exercise.

1. Eckhart Tolle teaches that putting our attention on our inner energy body (putting our attention inside of our bodies on the aliveness there) will bring us back to the Present moment, back to our True Nature. Start with putting your attention inside of your hands (you might feel tingling; that's the aliveness in the body), then put attention inside of your feet, arms and legs, and the rest of the body – focus on inside of those areas. Then put attention on the whole inner body. Do it now if you like, until you feel peace, aliveness, or quiet arise. Keep some of your attention there all day long if you can.

2. Pema Chodron a Buddhist teacher, invites us to label a thought, "thinking" and move back into giving attention to the out-breath. Notice that thinking stops.

3. Mooji, a heart-opening spiritual teacher, invites us to put our 'head in our heart'. Do it now and see what it feels like. Do it often throughout the day. Osho, an Eastern Spiritual teacher taught a similar method of 'thinking below the head' or 'going headless'. When an upset happens, ask your mind to rest in your heart and 'think' from there. You can't love from the head/mind. Think of someone who bothers you, move your 'thinking' down to your heart and notice the change.

4. Look out into nature (a tree, the sky, water) and connect by putting your attention on your inner self and nature at the same time. This double-attention exercise taught by Guy Finley explains why we feel expansive when we look at the sky, and transcendent when we watch a sunrise or a sunset. What we see in the outer nature

catalyzes our own corresponding timeless, immense, still, inner nature. Do it now so you can see for yourself.

5. As taught by Ramana Maharshi, silently ask the question, "Who am I?" and wait quietly to be shown. Wait until peace or another state of wellbeing appears. The pathway may take you through painful feelings caused by identities (feel them until they disappear). This strategy will lead you back to your True Nature.

6. Mooji invites us to leave our mind at the door with our shoes. Also leave the past, the present, and the future there, too. Notice that a feeling of connection with something deeper inside of us appears. 'The Invitation' from Mooji guides us through this and is available at Mooji.com and other booksellers, or you can Google 'The Invitation' with Mooji (there are a few free versions on You Tube).

7. Mooji invites us to place our palms together (prayer position), raise our hands to our faces and say, "Thank you, thank you, thank you, thank you," until we feel peace arise. This concurs with what other Masters' say about palms together: the opposites merge into oneness, or the left hand and the right hand coming together equilibrate the opposites, unite the divided mind, and reveal the Undivided Nature. When the left (feminine) and the right (masculine) merge, we rise above the duality of male/female, or any other opposites into oneness where no problem exists because there are no opposites. I do this one every single day because I love the feeling.

8. Eckhart Tolle teaches a unique technique for coming into awareness and Presence that involves 'not thinking' from now.......................... until now. During that time, notice the heightened awareness that

replaces thought. Do it now and try to extend the time you pause (don't think) every time you do it.

9.   Eckhart, among others, also teaches the invaluable lesson of accepting 'what is' in this moment. If done completely without judgment, one can be transported to one's True, selfless, timeless, joyful nature very quickly. To practice this, think of something that bothers you about yourself. Ask yourself if you can accept it now. Wait for a release. If you can't accept it, ask if you can accept that you can't accept it. No pretending. This won't transport you to peace unless you take the time to do it. When an unacceptable situation appears, ask yourself if you can accept the unacceptable and see what happens inside of you. There is a part of us that IS pure acceptance of what is; has no resistance to what is. In the moment, we can't change what's going on, so acceptance brings about sanity. Sadhguru teaches that this moment is inevitable, and it is, so acceptance of it makes perfect sense. That doesn't mean we don't take right action whenever and wherever we can.

10. Having space for the other to be identified is another technique from Eckhart Tolle and Suzi Lula. If we are able to this, it provides instant relief and, if one is able to stay in that space, it's the space of non-judgment and, therefore, peace. Think of someone with 'bad' behaviour. Then simply give them space to do whatever it is they do. Notice that the space you give the other creates space in you.

11. Sadhguru teaches us to notice when we like or dislike someone, something, a condition, an event, or a situation and to remind ourselves that liking, and disliking are not acceptance of 'what is' and keep you from your True Nature. Ask questions to yourself such as, "Is it necessary to like or dislike?", "Will I be okay if I don't like or dislike?", "Can I still be me if I don't like or dislike?", and

"Can I operate in the world and get what I need even if I don't like or dislike?"

12. Byron Katie, extraordinary teacher of The Work, a self-inquiry method, invites us to ask ourselves, "Who would I be without that thought?" This question, when experienced fully, will take one to their True Nature. To see how this works, think poorly of someone – judge them right now – and then ask the question and see what happens inside of yourself.

13. Close your eyes and focus on the spine.

14. Put your full attention on your breath as it comes into the body, as it expands the body, and as it leaves the body. Notice that breath is life. Eckhart invites us to take as many conscious breaths as we can in a day. Do it while waiting in line-ups, at stop lights, while on hold on the phone and dedicate time every hour for one or two conscious breaths. It shifts the level of consciousness we operate from. Breath is so closely linked to life and aliveness. No breath, no life. Because it's so closely linked to life, it easily transports us to a higher level of consciousness: the level of consciousness that is close to reality. Eckhart reminds us to notice the preciousness of the air we breathe, how automatic breathing is, and how we are taken out of thinking when we are focussed on the breath. This is really amazing to experience. The ability to be taken out of negative thinking so easily is remarkable. This is the most simple and effective practice there is for coming back to the moment and getting calm.

15. Adyashanti, a spiritual teacher who practiced Zen Buddhism, suggests we sit quietly and ask, "Stillness are you here?"

16. Adyashanti also invites us to notice what's present at all times no matter what's going on. Whether the wind is blowing, someone is talking, a car is going by – notice what's always there behind the things that are going on. Awareness is always here and transports us to that peaceful place inside of us.

17. Eckhart invites us to look at any object and wait until we can feel the stillness in it.

18. Joseph Campbell teaches a way of the Native Americans: look at anything (a tree, a chair, etc.) and call it – "It." Then look at it and call it "Thou." Feel the difference. Refer to things as Thou rather than it. You can feel a shift into softness and reverence. This is so respectful to all of life.

19. Close your eyes, tilt your head slightly back and focus on the spot between the eyebrows (Sadhguru).

20. *A Course in Miracles* teaches an instant remedy for bringing oneself back to their True Nature: during an upset say, "This doesn't have the meaning I've given it." This is true because if there is an upset, the ego is imprinting itself onto whatever is happening. To practice this strategy, when an upset appears, get quiet and say it. Wait quietly and feel what happens.

21. Suzi Lula teaches a simple way to come into coherence: put one or both hands over your heart and ask to reconnect to the Divine.

22. Vernon Howard, an American spiritual teacher suggests we recognize that thoughts are not who we are, and when upsetting ones appear, to think of them as a radio station and turn them off by dismissing them (repeatedly if necessary), until peace and stillness appear. Give your 'radio station' (chattering mind) a name

when it turns on and won't turn off! Mine is called TGMM (there goes monkey mind).

23. Creation created us, therefore, feel this as you say it to yourself, "I am enough."

24. Byron Katie teaches a simple and beautiful method that reaches inside of us all the way to the core of who we are when she asks us to ask this question in any upset: "Am I okay?" Get very still and ask this question, wait, and you will notice that even in traumatic moments, we are always okay. That's because, at our core, we are at peace, unaffected by the outer world, and therefore, always okay. This is effective also because there is an immortal part of us, an unseen part of us that "Is in this world, but not of this world." That part is inside of us but not part of the seen physical world, it's part of our Being. While immortality is not readily apparent to us, if you do enough of this type of work, you will begin to feel a deep connection to the part of us that is immortal, has no fear, and is untouched by upsets.

25. When an upsetting thought arises, say to yourself, "There is a thought. I don't have to respond or react to it."

26. Do the HeartMath Quick Coherence® Technique

The Quick Coherence® technique was developed by and is a registered trademark of HeartMath.
https://www.heartmath.com

"Create a coherent state in about a minute with the simple, but powerful steps of the Quick Coherence® Technique. Using the power of your heart to balance thoughts and emotions, you can achieve energy, mental clarity and feel better fast anywhere. Use Quick

Coherence® especially when you begin feeling a draining emotion such as frustration, irritation, anxiety or anger. Find a feeling of ease and inner harmony that's reflected in more balanced heart rhythms, facilitating brain function and more access to higher intelligence."

The HeartMath Quick Coherence® Technique:

"Step 1: Focus your attention in the area of the heart. Imagine your breath is flowing in and out of your heart or chest area, breathing a little slower and deeper than usual.

Suggestion: Inhale 5 seconds, exhale 5 seconds (or whatever rhythm is comfortable).

Step 2: Make a sincere attempt to experience a regenerative feeling such as appreciation or care for someone or something in your life.

Suggestion: Try to re-experience the feeling you have for someone you love, a pet, a special place, an accomplishment, etc. or focus on a feeling of calm or ease."

Science has proven that these types of strategies cause coherence in our brains, but why not prove it to yourself – and use one or more of them every day!

27. Utter the words "Neti, Neti," with the realization that you have the power to override any ego state in the moment it appears. Neti neti is a Sanskrit word that means "not this" and "not that". It's an eastern philosophy that negates everything that is not Isness, Beingness, the Source, or Atman.

30 Second Parenting Strategy
Fear and the 'Bogeyman'

Dismissing a child's fear doesn't dismiss the fear.

If fear arises, it will fall away, *if you observe it instead of being drawn* **into it.**

Feeling fear from something that isn't real (like a thought) is fake fear.

There are higher levels of consciousness that hold us safely no matter what's going on. We can only know this level of consciousness when we challenge what we think is true. Until we are living from that fearless place, the strategies here will help children (and adults) release themselves from fear.

When my grandkids are scared of going downstairs to the laundry room by themselves, the conversation goes like this, "Grandma, will you come with me?"

I go with them the first few times, depending on their age, and ask them what they are scared of. They say things like a bad guy or a monster, so I ask them if they've ever seen one. If they say yes, I ask what it looks like and they usually don't know. These first few times are for the parent to gather information about the child's fears.

As taught by Guy Finley, we go through the house turning on lights and opening doors and cupboards and looking into the deepest and darkest corners, so we can see for ourselves what is there and what isn't there.

It always ends in relief and light-heartedness.

Later, when they are in bed and say they are scared and can't sleep, the same process is undertaken. Soon enough, they realize nothing is there without going to look.

After a few times, or when they get old enough, as Guy suggests, a wise parent would invite them to turn on the lights and go look for themselves. This powerful teaching transforms and empowers children to look at reality for themselves. More importantly, it begins to teach them to live life without made up fear.

Another effective strategy is that fear, if you feel it all the way through, it will disappear by itself. After I've gone with them several times and, we've done the exercise above, and they still ask if I'll come downstairs with them, I reply, "No honey, stand on the first stair and feel the fear. I promise if you do that the feeling will disappear. It can't last long because it's not real. Remember when we looked all over to see if we could find something to be scared of? Go ahead and feel the fear. Tell me when the fear is gone." They wait and feel the fear and then reply that the fear is gone, and they take a step down. "I'm scared again," they say. I say, "Okay, feel the fear, I promise it will go away. It always does if you feel it all the way 'til it's over." This goes on until they are laughing and at the bottom of the stairs. It's so powerful to realize that fear has to dissipate if you wait long enough to feel it instead of letting it run away with you, get bigger, and then be an unwelcome and more constant companion.

If they are still too scared to proceed very far, we go through the entire process of looking in nooks and crannies.

I still use this technique myself when I feel fear that I know is irrational.

30 Second Parenting Strategy
Consequences

Well, well, if it isn't the consequences
of my own actions showing up.

-Unknown

Every action has a consequence. Words, actions, and thoughts all have consequences.

To be clear, taking no action is an action in itself and has a consequence.

This is a principle by which the world operates, it's not anybody's idea. It is what is.

One could spend as much time pondering the idea of being fully responsible for the consequences of one's actions as they do on what the action is.

Isn't it true that we *have to* live with the consequences of our actions, whether we like it or not?

Action happens and then consequence follows.

This is best explained in a story. One day I was driving home with cruise control on so that I wouldn't speed. I thought I was doing the right thing. Then along came a Mercedes van behind me and tailgated me for a long way. There was only one lane, and I was convinced that I was right, and he was wrong. I was going the speed limit! That had to be right, right? Wrong. The reality is that he was tailgating and if I don't like it, it's my responsibility to turn off the road and let him pass.

It would have been right for me to pull off the road, but I couldn't see that clearly enough because the thought "I'm doing the right thing by going the speed limit," was occupying my mind.

I could have saved myself the discomfort of being tailgated. My action of not pulling off the road caused me the consequence of unnecessary discomfort. I finally came to my senses and pulled over to let them pass. Once I did, I felt all the stress leave me.

Teach your kids about consequences. Not in a punishing way, but like this:

— When it rains, it's wet outside. If we go outside without an umbrella, we will get wet. The action of going out in the rain has a consequence of getting wet.

— As taught by Guy Finley, if we speed (action), we will feel stress (consequence). The action of speeding has a consequence of feeling some stress for several reasons: it's against the law and we may get a ticket. It increases the chance of an accident because, as our speed increases, slow-down time reduces. Putting ourselves in increased danger causes stress.

— If we text while we drive (action), we will feel stress (consequence) because we innately know that driving needs our full attention to avoid damage, injury, or death. Show your kids a commercial that shows someone driving and texting with death as the consequence. Nothing wrong with dying: we're all going to do it, but do you want to do it now - in this way?

— If we eat too many tacos (action), we have extra padding on our hips (consequence).

— If we hand our test in on time (action), we don't have stress, don't fight with our parents, don't make up false excuses so we feel good inside (consequences). The action of handing the test in on time has the consequence of feeling more peaceful.

— If we do something for someone else and don't expect anything in return (action), then we feel fulfilled (consequence). The action of freely giving has the consequence of feeling fulfilled.
— When we complain to another person (the action), we don't feel good inside (the consequences). We also cement our identity that says it knows how everything should be done and, in the cementing, the ego will appear another day to cause more pain, so the consequences are far reaching.

Teach your kids to accept, or at least not complain about, the consequences because they are within everything we do. They are inescapable so it's a good idea to ponder them every now and then.

As it relates to parenting, every action you take has some effect on your child. Without judging yourself, remember that. The point is not to judge, but to come into awareness.

How to deal with kids who don't comply with healthy cohabitation requests, like doing chores, completing homework, being honest, etc.? Make the consequences as 'natural' or as close to the action as possible. If you go out when it's raining (the action), then you get wet (the consequence). The consequence is a natural extension of the action.

Deliver the child's consequences without punishment. Punishment won't help. Consequences will. If you feel upset when you talk to your child about consequences, tell them you need five minutes and ask them to take a few minutes to consider the issue, too.

Try to never hand out consequences when you're mad because you have to live with them (the child and their consequences).

Here are some examples of more natural consequences:

Action: doesn't finish homework.

Natural Consequence: gets school penalties. (That's okay, we don't need to get involved).

Action: is failing.
Natural Consequence: gets a tutor or fails. (That's okay, it doesn't require a fight).

Action: won't help with household chores.
Consequence: don't get to use household items.

Action: gets a speeding ticket with the family car.
Natural Consequence: pays for the ticket, doesn't get the car next time.

These are suggestion, only. In my own life, when my grandkids are rough with my work computer (action), I just go pick it up (consequence) and invite them to feel what they are feeling and not to take it out on anyone or anything.

30 Second Parenting Strategy
Discipline

No punishment is so terrible as prosperous guilt.
-William Ellery Channing

"Discipline issues are always as a result of an unmet emotional need in the child."

"The child, when they push our buttons, are exposing a need that has been unmet and unresolved within ourselves leaving us unable to meet an emotional need within the child."

-Dr. Shefali Tsabary
www.drshefali.com

Source:
https://www.youtube.com/watch?v=dIRmSe_KIh8

Dr. Shefali, is a popular mindful clinical psychologist and, author of many books including *The Conscious Parent*. How to apply what she teaches: when a child acts out and you over-react, understand that there is an issue in you that you need to heal in yourself. Ask yourself what is hurting, what is my wound? Ask what do I need? See what need you have, whether it's respect, kindness, etc. Heal it by giving yourself whatever you feel you need. If you feel you need respect, give it to yourself by thinking, speaking, and acting respectfully to yourself.

Then sit quietly and ask to see what the child needs.

When a child acts out and is too young to figure that out, use your wisdom to discover what it is they need. Help them get it.

Teach your children to tell you they need attention rather than acting out to get it. What they really want is to be natural and feel connected.

So, where in this is discipline? Gone. This is parenting without using discipline. The need for discipline disappears, and, in its place appears looking inward to discover and meet real needs, to learn together and to blossom together.

Imagine sitting down and discover unmet needs rather than disciplining a child. Hard to imagine. Easy and loving way to live.

You can give consequences without 'disciplining' the child. You'll feel better and they'll feel better.

30 Second Parenting Strategy
Trade Perfection for Peace

Peace is perfection.

Wanting perfection causes stress, so, giving up perfection is giving up stress.

Perfection, as defined by the mind doesn't exist. Have you ever encountered a 'perfect' person who stayed perfect after you talked to them for a few minutes/hours?

What to watch for to give yourself relief from being identified with 'perfection':

— Criticizing a child for their behavior (instead of doing your own work on what it brings up in you, and, helping them do their work).
— Judging anyone or anything (including your body).
— Feeling tense while watching your kids perform at school or during sports or any other activity such as playing with other kids.
— Telling others 'how to do it' but feeling like a boss or know-it-all.
— Inserting yourself anywhere (in other people's business, such as in other people's conversations or by giving others unsolicited advice).
— You are feeling compelled by uneasiness to straighten the magazines (or anything else).

When you notice someone or something is 'not perfect', say one of these phrases to yourself:

"Perfection won't make me happy because it doesn't exist."

"What I think of as perfection is just compulsion."

30 Second Parenting Strategy
Making Peace with Problems

You know you've grown a lot as a parent when you watch
your kid lick something in public and
think, "Eh. He's licked worse."
-Popular saying by many.

Guy Finley teaches a simple strategy to take upsetting entanglement with the other's problems away in a heartbeat.

Think of someone who has a problem that upsets you. (Your child, a colleague, a partner, the grocery store clerk, a relative, a friend, the neighbor, etc.). For example, if the clerk didn't smile at you, if your partner didn't thank you, if your child burps, eats dirt, This strategy is not suggesting you take no action. It's saying do the strategy so you don't overreact and can take action that doesn't cause you stress.

Close your eyes and dissolve yourself from their problem. Imagine cutting the 'strings' or 'ties' from you to their problem.

Wait until you feel some distance and then from your heart, wish them the best. In our true hearts, we do wish the best for anyone and everyone, even if they've hurt us. How we know that to be true is that if they were to suffer a trauma of some kind, or be on their deathbed, our natural instinct would be to drop our nonsense and have compassion for them.

It's *natural* to wish someone the best.

After you've wished them the best, check back inside of yourself to see how you feel about them to see what's changed. If there is no change, do the exercise again, a bit slower.

Use this any time you feel upset about your child and their problem (or anyone else). You will feel differently about them, calmer, clearer, and your natural impulse to love will arise. You will also notice that your focus changes to the person not the problem. Ironically, the solution to the problem will likely appear or your annoyance from it will disappear. In any case, if you need to take action, it will come from a calmer place.

30 Second Parenting Strategy
Judging and Criticizing

Dissolve the judge and what's left is joy.

Judging or criticizing doesn't make you better than the other, doesn't make you smarter or wiser, won't make you or the one you are judging into a better person, and will never prove you are right.

Judging and criticizing just proves we are unconscious.

Refuse to do it.

When you are criticizing the other: notice it and stop, either mid-thought, or mid-sentence and re-group yourself with a conscious breath (pay attention to the breath entering the body, feel your body expand and then contract, pay attention to the breath leaving the body; repeat several times). It's impossible to think when your full attention is on the breath (as taught by Eckhart Tolle). If you take your attention away from the judge, you stop it. It needs your attention to exist.

We judge to put ourselves in a position of power, or, to feel 'better than', but **trading power for peace is a good decision.**

Sara Wiseman teaches a beautiful strategy to bring you into your heart: when you look at another human being and judgment happens, ask yourself if you could have compassion for them, or accept them instead.

Another strategy is to notice when you begin to judge or criticize yourself, another, or a situation, is to watch the inner judge and how it acts. Become the impartial observer. Notice how you feel inside.

Remind yourself that judging is not helpful in any way.

Notice that judging is insane and can't cause wellbeing to anyone.

This doesn't mean that we don't make judgments about practicality and daily life. This doesn't mean we let others hurt us. It means we get clear enough to make good decisions that are based on clarity not 'The Judge' inside of us who is always biased and punishing.

When the other is judging or criticizing you: can you see the other is identified when they are criticizing you? Use the opportunity to notice what's going on inside of you. Give what the other is saying (the one who is criticizing you) no attention; put your attention inside of yourself and watch and feel without speaking. The upset you feel as a result of feeling criticized will dissolve and take the stress with it.

The other person can go on being miserable, but you want to feel natural inside of yourself. The way to do that, as taught by many, including David Hawkins in his book *Letting Go*, is to keep feeling the feelings inside and that dissolves them. Nothing could be more simple or difficult at the same time. If you do it, freedom, release, and peace are the result.

30 Second Parenting Strategy
"I need a moment."

*"If your kids are giving you a headache, follow
the directions on the aspirin bottle, especially the
part that says keep away from children."*
— *Susan Savannah*

Suzi Lula teaches an on-the-spot relationship-changing technique to be used in a conversation that's working up some tension or confusion. In the moment an upset begins to appear, tell the other, "I need a moment." This dissolves, or at least decreases, big emotions that lead to bigger, unwanted words and actions.

When you 'take a moment' it gives you time to calm yourself so you can respond rather than react. As Suzi says, it also teaches children to learn patience if they have to wait a moment – which is helpful when they are so accustomed to instant gratification and instant answers from us.

www.suzilula.com

Parenting Differently

Where ignorance is our master,
there is no possibility of real peace.
-Tenzin Gyatso, the 14ᵗʰ Dalai Lama

It is essential to understand that none of us could have parented (or done anything else) differently than we did. If we could have done it differently, we would have. My father began teaching me this many years ago when I would complain about how someone was behaving. No one can operate above the level of consciousness that they are at.

If you're thinking about your parenting mistakes as you read this, use Blessing Mistakes for yourself: say and feel the truth of this statement, "I matter more than my parenting mistakes." Remind yourself that all people matter more than the mistakes they make. Then make your parenting mistakes right, as best as you can (that usually means apologize).

While it's true that we can't do differently until we know differently, it is time for a different way – for the sake of our own wellbeing and the wellbeing of our kids.

Instead of judging and then berating yourself if you feel you've made a misstep as a parent, use your favorite 30 Second Parenting Strategy on yourself to give you relief. That's more constructive and will leave you feeling happier and more available to your child.

Even after reading this book and using the 30 Second Parenting Strategies, at times, we are all going to lose patience, snap at a child, bribe and criticize them. The difference, you will notice, is that you are aware that you are acting in a way that doesn't serve you or them and you will want to use one of the strategies right away to bring yourself relief. Or, noticing will be enough to come back to sanity.

No one wants to hurt a child. When we do, we suffer and so do they. With this work, we reduce/end stress in so many areas of our lives and in our children's lives.

What We Do Right as Parents

They say it takes a village. Where
can I get directions to this village?
                              -www.rookiemoms.com

1. We look for ways to be better parents.
2. We try to provide our kids with a better life than we had.
3. We try to provide them with what we believe all their needs are: love, a roof over their heads, clothing, food, activities for fun, personal growth, and education.
4. We truly want the best life possible for them.
5. We play with them.
6. We try to guide them towards fulfillment.

The Mistakes We (Don't Mean To) Make as Parents/People

Never lend your car to anyone
to whom you have given birth.
— Erma Bombeck

As I've mentioned, it's important to understand that when we make a mistake, we are innocent in our ignorance. We can't operate from a higher level of understanding until we HAVE one.

At the same time, staying ignorant of our misunderstandings keeps upsets in perpetuity, so it's time for us to compassionately see the truth.

The 10 Mistakes We Don't Mean to Make as Parents

1. We disconnect (by punishing, blaming, and criticizing them) and try to 'fix' our kids (by punishing, blaming, and criticizing them), not knowing that if we help them connect to their True Selves, they will not just fit into life, but they will find joy in it.
2. We focus on things that can't make us happy.
3. We 'dump' and 'unload' on our kids and others as though it's our right. Where did we get the mistaken idea that everyone is here to please us and do everything our way? Dumping, complaining, and unloading have become second nature in a society that has never had more conveniences, comforts, and opportunities.
4. We think the other (our kids, partner, friends, strangers, gas station attendant, etc.) or a situation (work, the weather, the government's laws, etc.) causes our upsets when the truth is

that our own beliefs (that we are mostly unaware of) cause our upsets. This is provable and powerful because if the upset lies within, the cure does too. We don't have to rely on anyone else to bring ourselves back to our peaceful nature.

5. We take our thoughts, ideas, opinions, and beliefs as absolute truths. Most of them are prejudices for the benefit of one person, a few people, or even many, but not all. Pure intelligence serves all. Each of us has pure intelligence inside of us – no exceptions.

6. We blame kids and others instead of blossoming them.

7. We think stress is normal when it's a sign that we are out of harmony with truth.

8. We want our kids to be our own imperfect idea of perfection.

9. We punish kids because we don't know another way to get them to comply with what we think is best for them and for us. We mistakenly think that if the child is acceptable, we are acceptable. If they act out, we look bad, so we punish them to make them acceptable. **In that way, we punish the child because its best for us.** We never stop to consider what we really look like when we punish someone. We intuitively know that punishment is inherently wrong every single time we see it happening or do it to someone else. We think punishment corrects the child into acceptability, but really, it disconnects them from us, and it disconnects them from their Inner Wisdom because they begin to believe punishment corrects behavior. What corrects behavior is to see that the behavior is not serving anyone. What sees that is our True Nature, a higher level of consciousness that resides within. We can discover that for ourselves, and then, point to it if anyone else wants to see it within themselves. Our kids are counting on us to see it and teach it to them.

10. We think controlling kids will make them into good kids but, as Eckhart Tolle teaches, it's helpful to find the middle ground

between interfering and allowing. Too much control is the cause of rebellion.

Remember, none of us wants to hurt our kids or teach them ways of being in the world that don't work. If we knew another way, we'd have done it.

These truths are not hard-hitting, they are sanity-saving. **The sooner we abdicate the throne of ignorance, the sooner we ascend to the throne of wisdom.**

If there ever was a time to recall this old adage, it's now: THE TRUTH WILL SET YOU FREE.

The truth never hurts. Beliefs do. If you feel upset by what you've read, your beliefs are being challenged. Thank them for trying to help you, dismiss them, and keep reading - towards the truth. This is not a judgment against anyone, it's an education meant to inform and change us to how we want to be.

I'm not inviting you to believe anything written in these pages. I'm inviting you to test every single thing here for yourself to see if it's true.

Making the Right Connections

It's good that we've sent people into outer space,
but now it's time to send them into inner space.
Valuable discovery happens there, too.

The 30 Second Parenting Strategies in this book take us out of a fundamental mistaken idea that we learned as kids: we are separate - disconnected from ourselves, from others, and from what created us. The disconnection is why we believe there is something wrong with us. We may have a flaw or two, but that doesn't have to define us, OR become our focus.

If we believe we are flawed, we believe the way to happiness is to fix ourselves. We focus on fixing the flawed human being, not on the 'Being' part of the human. We focus on what's wrong, not on how to re-connect to the parts of ourselves and others that aren't flawed in any way: the innermost Being – that part of us that is like a child but also contains limitless and natural wisdom. In that state problems don't appear as problems. Right action is always taken. While that seems idealistic (and it is until one comes into full understanding of how the Universe actually operates), why would it not be possible?

There is another problem with the idea of 'fixing'. Look at all the 'fixing' we've done. It doesn't work. That's because we don't need fixing and neither do our kids. We need connecting. If we deeply connect, the focus on separation and flaws, dissolves into naturally being who we are; pressure, pretense, and the underlying sense of unease that so subtly disturbs our peace disappears.

The 'Being' is the inner part of the human that is connected to everything and as a result, can't fight anymore.

Kids need guidance towards their pure inner intelligence; they don't need fixing. We need the same thing.

There is no amount of fixing that will connect a human being to their inner treasures. If peace comes from within (and that's the only place we can experience anything, so it must come from within), then we have to find ways to look into ourselves and connect to that part of us.

We've all experienced what deep connection feels like whether it's with our kids, our loved ones, animals, or even nature. That's how we know this to be true even if it's not at the forefront of our consciousness: troubles dissolve when we feel connected.

Think about what happens when we pet the dog or cat. We feel connected and troubles disappear. Anyone who has owned an animal knows this to be true.

When deep connection is felt, troubles fall away.

We are mostly focussed on what doesn't give us connection: our jobs, our homes, our status, our body image, etc. Said more simply, we are connected to how we look, how others see us, how much money we have, etc. A child is not connected to those things and therefore, is closer to their Natural Selves. They don't 'believe' any of those things will solve problems or make them happy. They don't seek happiness outside of themselves because it comes naturally to them. Connection to material things keeps us forever in the no-exit loop of wanting and getting and then wanting more; like a rabbit endlessly chasing the carrot around the racetrack; never catching it. We want a different body, a better job, a nicer house. Kids don't want those things BECAUSE they aren't what keep us connected or happy.

Another example of connection is when we are immersed in creating something; doing something we love, or we are 'in the zone'. We don't usually think that we are connecting while we are creating something, but the feeling of connection is exactly what is happening. For example, if you love photography, when you're taking pictures in nature, you feel connected to nature, to the camera, and to what you're doing; it's all seamless. In those states, troubles disappear. If you're a runner, or enthusiast of any type, you know that total engagement/connection eliminates 'thinking' and problems.

That's because we're immersed in the moment, and it's a Universal Law that when we are fully in the moment, there is nothing wrong. That's the gift of Presence. Presence is a state of being where connection is automatic and 'thinking' stops (unless, as taught by Guy Finley, thinking is for practical purposes like planning, revelation – like doing this work, or creativity).

Simple logic taught by Eckhart Tolle: The past doesn't exist in the Present moment. That's easy enough to see if you sit with it for a moment; can the past be here right now, in this moment? Of course not.

In that same way, the future can't exist in this moment. If the past and future don't exist right now, then what is here right now? Sit and see. Close your eyes and ask yourself, "Does the past exists right now?" Feel what that feels like. Ask, "Does the future exist right now?" Do it until you feel calmness, spaciousness, or stillness arise. When we are connected to right now, this moment, we've arrived at a 'portal to peace', as Eckhart Tolle says. **Stressful thoughts can't exist in the state**

of Presence. Most of us have minds that talk to us endlessly, mostly about past or future. All of that stops when Presence arises.

We care about it this because we all want peace, and this is one of the easiest practices towards that place.

The mind was meant to be a magnificent tool for us, not an obsessing, relentless, sometimes eerily dark, task master.

You've noticed by now that the mind is capable of extremely negative or even violent thoughts about ourselves, and others. When that happens, the mind is randomly vomiting unconscious bits of information that it absorbed in the past.

We've all seen and absorbed abusive, sick, twisted, or violent ideas through television, the internet, or in real life. That information is stored in the unconscious mind/body even though it's not in our conscious awareness. These thoughts are illogical, uninformed, and in most cases would never be acted on. While they are disturbing, these kinds of thoughts do not make you bad or mean that something is wrong with you, and, they have no importance or meaning to you as a Being.

Different bits of that kind of information rise up into the conscious mind and become disturbing thoughts. There is no need to connect to that part of ourselves.

If you'd like to see how crazy the mind truly is, Osho offers an exercise that shows you why you can't trust your own mind. Not trusting your own mind means that when you have a thought that doesn't serve you, you don't need to trust it. Sit for fifteen minutes and write every single thought that arises. You will see that the mind, as it is, makes no sense. For that reason, you can assure yourself that random thoughts that are dark or crazy can be dismissed, not given attention; they are coming from a part of the mind that has had free reign on your life – until you do this work. Then you become the Master of your own mind and it works for you, not against you.

Keep using any of the strategies that give you relief when you have an upsetting thought that won't leave you alone.

There is never connection in a divided mind.

The Masters I refer to are in Unity Consciousness which is the same nature you and I have inside of us, but isn't our operating system yet. That state of existence is peaceful and has no judgment in it. That is easily understood with someone we deeply love; there can be an absence of personal judgment and, instead, a feeling of deep connection. That is the constant state of the Masters.

While we are divided, in duality, seeing through the lens of good and bad and all other opposites, it is a guarantee that our thoughts could send us for psychiatric help if we didn't know what was going on. I'm not supporting behaviors and actions that do not serve us, I'm simply pointing out that being attached to good and bad causes a lot of stress. For me, even though my mom experienced schizophrenia, with the help of the Masters, I began to see that my violent or crazy thoughts came from absorbing bits of information in the past and from identifying with ideas like I am good. If one believes they are good, they also believe they are bad and believing one is bad generates evil thoughts.

YOU ARE NOT BAD. That's not who you are when you have an ugly thought. The thoughts come from learned garbage. There are no such thoughts in your True Nature. You are purity itself without knowing it yet. You are love itself without knowing it yet. The way to know it is to do this inner work and it will reveal itself to you.

As Sri Nisargadatta taught, "The discovery of who you are comes through the discovery of who you are not." That is relevant to this work because a lot of what we do is to uncover false information in the mind, and then it becomes useless and powerless.

During deep connection, the sense of 'I' disappears and yet we competently continue on doing what we're doing. This happens because we are out of our lower nature (I, me, mine) and when that happens, we automatically connect to that which is so much larger than us: we are connected to whatever created this whole Cosmos - the earth, the trees and us remarkable human beings.

The sense of 'I' is unnecessary, but we don't know that. The sense of 'I' is from memory. That makes no sense whatsoever. That equates to: I am my memory – that's who I am.

The sense of 'we' works better, but we have a limited understanding of that, too.

Simple logic: 'We' is truer than 'I' because there is one 'I' and many 'we's'.

With deep connection the world stops revolving around us and totally involves us.

Applying this truth to our lives gives us clear direction: when we're upset, we need to remind ourselves that we've disconnected. We're involved with the painful 'I' and its painful story, and worse, giving it our full attention, believing every upsetting thought and disturbing emotion instead of reconnecting with our Being. We were meant to give our attention to this moment and that's all. When we do, we become clear about what would serve all in any situation.

When we lose the sense of 'I', we don't lose ourselves, we gain everything (peace).

Every strategy in this book is to enhance connection (we), and dissolve disconnection (I, me, mine), and that ends troubles. If you feel alarmed at the idea of dissolving the lower-natured self (I, me, mine, the ego), ponder this: can it be any worse than what's going on with me now? What's left after the dissolution of pain-causing 'I'deas, is blissful higher-nature happiness. **An 'I'dea is the ego having a thought. 'I'deas' aren't related to creativity or practicality, they are related to ego-based, self-centered notions that care about the lower-natured self that doesn't know how to care.**

True Expression

No dumping allowed.

Another fundamental mistake we make as human beings is that we believe we must express our upsets. What if 'watching' the upset that's happening inside of us was another option that actually dissolved the upset, taking with it the need to berate, belittle, criticize, or explode all over another human being (or ourselves)?

Since expressing our upsets involves hurting others 99% of the time and ourselves 100% of the time, maybe it's time to rethink that.

We are so used to expressing negatively during upsets (we blame, holler, frown, etc.) that we think it's just the way it is when it happens. We also believe, every single time we're upset, that we're right to be upset. But, if we begin to notice how we feel when we're in those states, it's pretty clear how 'off' we feel inside. When we are truly doing the 'right' thing, there is a solid and gentle knowing that accompanies it; there is no 'off' feeling. When we feel off or upset, that's the indicator that we're out of sync with life, not that we're right.

It's not normal to express an upset except to rid ourselves of the excess energy we've just created with whatever belief is negatively operating us.

It is normal to express the built-up excess energy in a way that won't hurt us, or another – and that's only true until it's normal to 'watch' the upset – and that's only true until the connection is so deep that

nothing can shatter the peace in the first place, then there is no excess negative energy to express.

Our True Nature is untouchable and untouched by negativity.

One day in the future, humanity will understand this idea and it will be common after experiencing an upset to vigorously move the body or quietly watch the upset inside of ourselves until it dissolves: both effectively ridding us of excess energy.

Purposely shaking the body to get the excess energy out is a good method. Any vigorous movement is helpful; dancing around the kitchen while banging pots and pans works, or, hitting the pillow as hard as you can without hurting yourself releases the negative energy. It might appear crazy at first, but you will see, over time, that getting the energy out in ways other than shooting it out towards others actually works to rid yourself of the anger in the moment, and then you can do your own inner work on the issue to help it dissolve. Expressing the negativity towards another or towards self brings the trouble back again and again because the deeper issue that caused the build-up of the negative energy in the first place hasn't been honestly addressed. The deeper issue is that we have something out of harmony inside of us and the upset moment is happening for us to bring what's out of harmony into our awareness, so we can come back *into* harmony.

In an attempt to help trauma victims at accident scenes, many first responders try to stop the shaking (in my own experience), when it would be most beneficial to shake the excess energy out of the body, not let it store inside where it disrupts the body's systems.

When negative energy (a belief) stores in the body (instead of dissipating as a result of dealing with the cause) it results in aches, pains, illness, and disease. Vernon Howard says that if people knew the true cause of sickness, they'd get up and walk out of the hospital. Sadhguru says that 70% of our diseases are caused by beliefs. If you do this work, you will begin to see aches and pains disappear along with some illnesses. Beliefs cause stress. Stress causes disease.

As Eckhart Tolle teaches, if you watch ducks in nature, after a skirmish, they vigorously shake their bodies and then peacefully go on their way. We might not be ducks, but we do naturally shake in a dramatic situation for a good reason.

If we were able to rid ourselves of the excess energy, we'd lose the seeming need to take that negative energy out on the other or on ourselves (judge self, and/or give in to destructive behaviors like addiction).

How we express our upsets has consequences. We usually don't like them.

It is also sometimes necessary to look deeper into the upset to resolve the issues that are causing the upset. Many of the strategies in this book help with that.

Why We Get Upset - The Truth About Beliefs

"A belief is a thought that can't be validated."
-Eckhart Tolle

It seems like beliefs are a good idea. It seems like that's how we make sense of the world. It seems like beliefs can be validated: for example, there *are* bad people in the world – that's a valid belief, isn't it?

When we examine beliefs closely, with the truth as our only goal, we discover something entirely different.

Let's examine this one together: 'There are bad people in the world'.

Using Byron Katie's work (www.thework.com), here's what I discovered when I put my belief through her process:

Is it true, 'There are bad people in the world?'
Yes.
Can I absolutely know it's true, that the thought, 'There are bad people in the world' is true?
Yes
How do **I react** when I believe the thought, 'There are bad people in the world'?

  — Concerned.
  — Frustrated.
  — Angry.
  — Judgmental.
  — Insistent: I feel the pressure of insisting there are bad people in the world.

— I think of the atrocities committed against humanity.
— I feel chocked up and tears come.
— My stomach feels like it's clenching.
— Images from the past that arise: being scared of being reprimanded.
— Images I see in the future: I wonder about the hope we have for humanity, I see images of war, of hurting each other, of forgetting about wellbeing as the priority.
— The more I think about it the more upset I get.
— I think I know what's good and what's bad. This thought gives me pause and I can see that when I was sick, I thought it was bad and yet it was the illness that sent me on my pathway of finding real and lasting relief from the stress I lived with – so what was bad became the best thing in my life. My awareness from doing this work right now is that I put a label on everything as good or bad when I don't know if every single thing that ever happened on the planet might look bad and end up good somehow – and it might happen in a way I can't know.
— What do I gain from believing this thought 'There are bad people in the world'? (This is a question that used to be asked often in The Work when I was attending Katie's School for the Work, but it's not asked so much anymore – I still use it all the time because it uncovers my formula for staying stuck in a belief). The gain if I believe there are bad people in the world: I'll know the right thing to do.
    o The belief that there are 'bad' people helps me know the right thing to do. That means my moral compass thinks it depends on others being bad, so I know how to be good.
    o That's what was hidden in the unconscious mind until the moment I did this work.

Who would I be without the thought 'There are bad people in the world'?

— If I could never think that thought, even while someone in front of me was, say, hitting a dog or doing something worse:
    o If I can't have that thought:
        ▪ I feel compassion rise up in me.
        ▪ I feel like I can take practical action and ask the person to stop, and if they don't, I can call for help.
        ▪ I feel relaxed (and am surprised by that).
        ▪ I feel relief.
        ▪ I feel loving towards the person even though they are misguided at the moment.
        ▪ I 'see' that they are identified with a belief, too and they are acting out of it.
        ▪ Tears come again, as they often do when I see the suffering that beliefs cause for myself and others.

The Turnaround to 'There are bad people in the world':

1. There are no bad people in the world (how might that be true or truer?)
    a. Their True Nature is goodness and they are acting out their beliefs, not their nature.
    b. They arrived as babies without badness.
    c. They are believing their thoughts and that's what making them act like that.

In The Work you find two more opposites to the original statement to complete the Turnaround.

The Work helped me see that the belief:

— IS what caused my stress (caused frustration etc.).

— **When I experienced the question, 'Who would I be without the thought?', I felt compassionate and had no stress. With the thought I felt a lot of stress. To me this is an important point because it proves that the belief itself causes the stress. It's more important for me to remain in the place of compassion. For one thing, I won't do anything inhumane while I'm in that state. For another, when someone else is doing something that doesn't serve or goes against another person, animal or the earth, I won't add to the problem – I might be clear and calm enough to truly help.**

— Showed me why I kept unconsciously believing the thought – it was my guide. (If I can see 'bad' in others, then I know how to be good – Ugh. What about the fact that our nature IS naturally good and harmless – I instinctively know what is good without needing a belief to confirm it).

— Is a faulty program that I am conforming to.

— Is like operating with a gavel: I'm right and that's final. My belief doesn't let me see anything else.

— When I'm lying in bed at night and think about bad people and get stressed out, it's proof that in that moment, since there are no bad people there, that the stress I feel is because of a thought I'm believing.

— I understand that I always need to take right action when I see harm happening (sometimes that's minding my own business and sometimes it's offering help). I can take right action without needing a belief telling me what right action is.

It's important to notice that kids operate without beliefs. Remember, they are not informed by things like skin color or status; they will play with you no matter what color you are or what job you hold. Kids don't start having hissy fits until they **believe** they want something that they don't get (just like us). A very young child doesn't have or need beliefs. They operate from their nature.

What is it that causes ways of being that we all love: kindness, honesty, generosity, etc.? Will *believing* we should be kind, honest, generous, etc. make us kind, honest, generous, etc.? We may intend to never hurt or holler at another person again, and we might even believe we won't, but it's a guarantee that we will until the belief that made us holler or hurt the other is dug out by the roots and examined for the troublemaker that it is – the belief will go on acting through us. Using my own example, the belief is one that I adopted in an attempt to help myself try to be a good person. It's just that it doesn't help me – it causes me tremendous stress.

We know that our True Nature doesn't act out against anyone. How we know that is when we are in natural states of compassion, authenticity, generosity, playfulness, etc. we are completely comfortable and wouldn't think of hurting ourselves or another. Those ways of being in the world always feel right. There is nothing 'off' about them. If there is an 'off' feeling with any of them, they are not natural to us, not part of our nature.

We don't have to believe in love for love to be true. Love is what's left, who we are, when we peel away beliefs.

Harmlessness is built-in to us, so 'morals', learning to be a good person isn't required.

With our hearts as our operating system, it's impossible to teach prejudice. Hearts are not informed by beliefs or prejudice. Our hearts operate on 'us'.

When we have beliefs (whether we consciously know them, OR, they are hidden in the unconscious mind) that's all we know to teach. It seems natural that if we have a belief, it's natural to teach it to our children.

Beliefs and prejudice are synonymous.

If we believe we are superior, even to one other human being (and we do), we will also have to believe someone is less than and we will teach our children that way of being in the world. That's prejudice. 'better than' and 'less than' are another pair of opposites that operate us. Prejudice isn't natural to us (remember kids don't register skin color, status, etc.). Prejudice is learned so it can be unlearned.

Our True Nature doesn't need to believe (insert a belief_____) to be okay in the world. Some examples are, I'm right, I'm smart, etc.

If we honestly don't have a belief, it can't be challenged or catalyzed inside of us because it doesn't exist inside of us.

We have two operating systems: our heads (beliefs) or our hearts (conscious awareness). Our heads divide and our hearts include.

It's normal to experience an upset if we're out of harmony with the laws by which the Universe operates. That's the only time we're ever upset, as taught by Guy Finley.

We can understand this better if we realize that we believe we are upset when something (as we see it) is out of order. The problem is that we are looking through our own 'I'deas (ego-based notions). We want *our* order to prevail, our justice to prevail. What happens when everyone wants something different, believes they are right? War. Can beliefs be right if they cause war? Are we meant to annihilate each other any time we don't agree?

Simple logic: If beliefs cause fighting, then not having beliefs causes peace.

We're not upset because of what someone did or said, or because of a situation or an event. We're upset because we are experiencing the effect of a belief that doesn't serve and is based on an old program running off course and on autopilot in our heads. The software that is running us is faulty. I don't need to believe in bad people for me to behave well. When we feel natural, we're in our nature. When we're in our nature, we know what to do and say without any pressure.

The programming (belief) needs to be interrupted to change it. Most of the strategies in The Kid Code are just that, gentle interventions!

We need to see that *the belief is not true.* 'Seeing' a belief is not true brings us back into harmony. Once we 'see' it, we no longer have to be it.

Beliefs are handcuffs.

Every belief is dedicated to proving itself right, not true.

Being sane is so much better than being right.

What we need is freedom from beliefs.

All stress comes from a learned or conditioned part of ourselves that sets itself up to be our guide, our inner authority, the one we think we should listen to – like, "I need respect." Might there be something else to listen to inside of us that's connected to this life we are? If I believe I need respect, and I don't get it – wham – the button in me is pushed and I get upset. I learned that respect is good. But, the problem is that I attach to respect and demand it of others in order for me to be okay. I cling to it as a strategy to make me happy. What if I'm okay without the respect of the other? What if I'm okay if the other disrespects me. Does their respect or disrespect define me? Can I be happy without it? Can I see how much stress wanting or not wanting those states causes me? We don't need to hook our star to the other's way of being.

Is This A Valid Belief: I am better than someone else?

Is it worth fighting over?

Can we prove that we are better than another? What's the proof?

If we believe we are better than someone else, that gives birth to the idea that someone is worse than us. We can't think we are better than another without thinking they are worse than us. From that we experience arrogance, self-righteousness, and dislike, or in its extreme forms, we experience hatred that drives us to violence. All of that coming from a belief that we are better than another.

We are not conscious of these beliefs. Becoming aware of them as they arise in your life takes away their power because they are not the truth.

The opposite of a belief is pure intelligence, and pure intelligence serves all.

Beliefs hide our intelligence.

Beliefs make us unintelligent.

Beliefs hide the truth.

It's not so difficult to understand that a belief is unnecessary, is not true, is unhelpful, is disruptive, etc. Just imagine for a minute if you didn't have any beliefs and the phone rings. You still pick it up and say hello. You still function just fine; you go to work, make meals, meet with friends, do the laundry. Just image that you can't be affected by the other respecting or disrespecting you – it's not even on your radar. They go on respecting or disrespecting and we stay calm and joyful. With no beliefs we function without stress - since it's the belief itself that's causing the stress.

Without beliefs, we wouldn't be empty-headed, we'd be full-hearted.

If we don't need to have beliefs, connect to, and be operated by them, how can we find out what to connect to?

We are already connected to our nature. Beliefs have obscured that.

There are many ways to get re-connected, as shared in the strategy called Diverting to Divinity. Doing the inner work in The Kid Code is a way to get re-connected. You probably know many ways yourself. Here's a few more:

— Go outside and stand on the ground.
— Stand in nature and absorb it.
— Ask, "What is the real, deep 'I' connected to, if not beliefs?" as taught by Eckhart Tolle.

Examples of some of the false beliefs we learn and then teach to our kids (through modelling or talking about), along with the truth are below:

Belief: Life is a struggle.
Truth/The Way the World Really Works: What we 'think' about life based on beliefs is the real struggle. There is no struggle when we are connected.

Belief: Life is unfair.
Truth/The Way the World Really Works: Creation has everything worked out and we can't see it while our True Nature is obscured by

beliefs. **Life has been operating for a long time without our opinion.** Justice is not our job, it's Creation's job. Actions are automatically taken care of with pre-existing consequences. Justice unfolds without our help or opinion. This is called karma. Karma means action (all actions have built-in consequences) whether we see them or not.

Another way to look at this is, as Byron Katie says, life is happening for us not to us. That means every upset is for the purpose of us to come out of unconsciousness and into consciousness.

Belief: Others should be nice.
Truth/The Way the World Really Works: The other acts based on their beliefs until connection to Creation is complete. The other may act mean because they believe that if they are mean and angry that's how they bring about order or get their way. How the other acts is not our business. How we respond is our business. We don't need the other to be nice if we are solid inside of ourselves. Others being nice won't take us to our peaceful Inner Nature. Truth will. When we are connected, we can't see through eyes that see or are affected by the identities of nice or mean. Our true eyes see out of our hearts even when the other is mean. Ironically our own transformation towards peace can affect the other positively, and their negative energy can dissipate instead of gathering more steam when a belief has been catalyzed in them.

Belief: If we please others, we'll be safe and happy.
Truth/The Way the World Really Works: Notice that the more we try to please people, the more upset we get with people. Notice that pleasing others has never caused us to be safe or happy, or even get what we really want, which is peace. Being our own genuine, honest selves really pleases others. You know this to be true because you love those qualities in others. Pleasing others is their job; we are unable to

go inside of them and make them connect with their inner wise Self. Pleasing us is ours.

There are many beliefs that become the CEO in our minds without us even knowing it's happening – until we have so much stress that we feel pushed into looking deeper at what's really causing it. If we had a CEO at work like the one in our heads, we'd quit.

Consider this: during an upset, the only reason I'm upset is because I am believing a thought about myself that is being challenged by what someone said or did. Part of that belief is, "I'm not like that." In my twenty plus years of experience studying and working with the mind, I've seen that I have every single behavior I see in the other. This has been confirmed by the Masters and many others. Some of our beliefs will be more latent in us and some more active, but they're all there. You can prove it to yourself AND more importantly, you can dissolve in you what you see in the other that you don't like. Are we willing to see if it's true or not? We can do this work and experience freedom or defend our beliefs and feel upset – that's the two choices we have.

Being ourselves, without needing to be anything else is amazing all by itself. We have joy built into us, just like a child does. We are wired to experience wisdom. **The cause of joy is Beingness, not beliefs**. The effect of doing simple inner work is inner peace. A happy ending (a happy Being) is inevitable when you know how the Universe operates.

During an upsetting thought, some good questions to ask yourself are:

— "Do I need to believe what I'm thinking?"
— "Right now, how would I feel without this belief?"
— "Is this belief making me happy?"

30 Second Parenting Strategy
I Am That

Everyone is an image of yourself –
your own thinking coming back to you.
                                        -Byron Katie

Darn it.
                        -Me

This is one of my favorite strategies and I use it a few times a day when I'm with kids. It's never failed to bring calmness to all of us.

When I am the adult in charge of my grandchildren, as soon as one child accuses another ("You're mean!"), we stop what we are doing, and everyone present (including me) closes their eyes and finds a time when they acted in that same way. We wait quietly for a situation to arise into our awareness where we behaved that way, and then feel the feelings that come with it.

My grandchildren were very young the first time I tried this with them. In the early hours of the morning, four of them came into my bedroom and playfully jumped on the bed. Before long the fun turned to fighting and I asked them all to sit with me and close our eyes. Ruby was really little, so she peeked one eye open to see what was happening. I blew a kiss at her and blinked my eyes. She closed her eyes and we all looked inside of ourselves. I will never forget how surprised I was: when we all turned inward, the energy turned peaceful. I didn't really expect it to work like it did. Every single one of them could find a time when they were mean. Once the discovery was made, it was time to play again, and the energy was back to natural.

From that day forward, I've have invited them to do this work with me every time upsets break out and it's like magic. Chaos to calmness in a minute. Joy!

To anchor a child is in this once you see an upset start:

1. Invite them to come and do the work with you.
2. Tell them you'd be happy to do the work on any issue because you want freedom, too.
3. If you don't know the issue (didn't hear it), ask them to explain so you can get clarity. After you hear what they have to say, make the issue as concise as possible by boiling it down to one or a few words.
4. Ask everyone to close their eyes as you close yours and ask them to see where they were (insert the issue). Ask them to feel what it feels like inside of them when they behave that way.
5. Wait quietly for about 15 seconds and then share what you found. Share how it feels to act in that way.
6. Ask each child to share the event and how it felt inside when they acted that way.
7. Notice the energy has shifted from upset to calm immediately once each person has gone inside to look at their own behavior.

Another way to ask this question to yourself is, "Where in my life have I behaved in that same way?" If we get still, the images will come to show us that we have behaved in the exact same way.

There will naturally be uncomfortable feelings as you 'see' where you are what you are accusing another of, usually for a few seconds or longer. That is called 'conscious suffering', as taught by Guy Finley.

When we 'see' and feel (consciously suffer) it, the behavior coming from a belief loses its power.

Notice that we are upset with another for behaving in the same way we do, and we don't like it in them or in us.

This exercise is based on the ancient teaching that the outer world reflects the inner world. If we see something we don't like in the outer world, going inward and seeing where we have been/done the same *is* the way out of it.

Many self-awareness teachers have taught this pointer to peace down through the ages, most notably, Sri Nisargadatta and Byron Katie.

We are scared of looking inside of ourselves, and for that reason, often want to resist this type of work because we don't want to be seen as 'bad'. If the behavior is in there, ignoring it won't keep it away. Looking to see the reality, *that we are what we accuse another of,* sets us free of the behaviors we don't like.

Doing this exercise, or any other self-inquiry work, doesn't make us bad; it makes us honest, which explains the old saying, *The Truth Will Set You Free.*

It's is the most amazing thing to see a 7-year-old do this work. When we do this together, the negative energy and conflict is discharged immediately. The first time I tried it, I was astounded that they could grasp the concept, and that they would agree to do it.

Little kids know the truth without knowing they know.

Sometimes they will say, "I don't want to do that, Grama!" and I reply, "This is the way I know to change how we feel, and I know we don't want to feel like we do right now." If there is any more resistance to this form of conscious conflict resolution, I say, "Okay, you don't have to do it; it means the hurt comes back again until you see the truth. I don't want to hurt, and I know you don't want too either. You choose."

This strategy discharges negativity. Everybody wants that.

Learn this and then teach your children. You will have several opportunities every single day. When you are able to experience the relief in this exercise yourself, that's when you will be able to anchor your child or any adult in it.

There is a huge relief as a parent to use a tool like this. It doesn't matter who blames whom. We can always use the opportunity to free ourselves because every human being has every behavior, some more prevalent than others.

My granddaughter, Jess, at age 10 is amazingly good at this strategy. She looks to see where she has behaved in the way she's accusing the other of, feels how awful it feels to behave in that way, and then takes her understanding deeper. If a child of 10 can do this work and feel peace, I look forward to seeing what her life will be like! If a 10-year-old can do that, what are we waiting for?

30 Minute Parenting Strategy
The Work of Byron Katie

Suffering is optional.

-Byron Katie

Byron Katie, a humorous, light-hearted, and very clear human being has helped millions of people world-wide find peace of mind no matter what problems they face. She lives a life of joy "for no reason" with no stress. While that seems impossible to imagine, she is living proof that it is not only possible, but likely, if we do this work.

Her system is called 'The Work' and invites us to put our upsetting thoughts on paper and then question them (there is a download for free called the 'Judge Your Neighbor Worksheet' from her website with both video and written instructions: www.thework.com/dothedk. php). I shared an example of doing The Work on one of my beliefs in the section titled: Why We Get Upset: The Truth About Beliefs.

Once you fill in the one-page worksheet, you ask the 4 Questions and the Turnarounds to each statement you've written while sitting quietly with each question to see what is true for you.

Katie offers a nine-day school, weekend classes, Turnaround House (a 28-day addiction program), and the end of suffering as we know it. Don't miss her work. It is a simple and amazingly effective tool to bring calmness, clarity, and practical action back into our lives.

I love the freedom that her works gives me so much that I've been to her School for The Work four times and her Turnaround House once. It turned me around!

30 Second Parenting Strategies
The Turnaround

The work is checkmate for the mind.
-Byron Katie

This method, taught by Byron Katie, takes a negative thought, and invites us to find out how the opposite of the thought is true or truer. When I don't have time to go through her entire process, I use this part of it.

If your child has behaved in a way that is upsetting to you, likely you will have a negative thought about them. For example, if a child is behaving in a mean way and you have the thought "S/he's mean," before speaking or acting towards the child, take a moment to consider the opposite: "S/he's kind," and see where that's true or truer. Find three events where it was true that the child was kind. If you are blaming or accusing your child, this strategy will soften you and your response to them. You will be grateful for doing this – for your own wellbeing.

If action is required immediately and there isn't time to turn the thought around, like if a child is hitting another child, you can do the work later.

This strategy works because it equilibrates the opposites and brings us into a neutral place that results in words and actions that have less painful consequences.

If you use this often, you will notice the stressful energy dissipates instantly.

Even when you have a negative thought about yourself, it's good to use this method to bring you back to peace. If you are thinking, 'I am a bad parent,' turn it around to 'I am a good parent' and find three examples of when that statement was/is true.

An example is:

Negative Thought: I am a bad parent.
Turnaround: I am a good parent.
How is the turnaround true?
3 examples:
I give lots of time to them.
I support their decisions.
I teach them these strategies.

30 Second Parenting Strategy
The 'Y'

"The only crisis we've ever had is an Identity crisis."
                                    -Guy Finley

That means that all upsets are caused by believing something that is not true.

When an upset happens, you've come to the "Y" in the road and the path you take will determine whether the upset amps up or down. The question is, do we want to take control of our emotions, or let them take control of us?

There are two possible paths to take in an upset.

In a moment of upset, an identity (an idea, not your True Nature) has you in its grip.

If we take the path laid out by the identity, (the 'human thinking compass' whose favorite position is, 'I'm right' and I'm about to prove it) we will feel the upset escalate and a bit of trouble becomes a lot of emotional upset. That's not good for our wellbeing.

If we don't do the work on an upset, we will experience more misery down the road as it reincarnates itself. If we do the work on an upset, the patterns we carry inside of ourselves change and we no longer unconsciously manifest the same issue and upset because we've worked it out. An upset is designed to bring harmony into our lives, and it will if we do this work.

If you give the identity any power, it will dictate what you are about to say, do and feel (all under the heading of hurting and/or suffering). If you give the identity authority over you, you are not fighting for yourself; you are fighting against yourself.

If you want to take the other path (the path of your True Nature), you can say this to the identity (the upset), "You have no authority over me." The identity has no choice but to let go in favor of your True Nature because all identities have no real power.

When you teach this to a child, draw a picture of a "Y" and explain that they can end their hurt by saying, "No, you're not the boss of me," to the upset they feel. Use your hand and fingers to make a "Y" and ask them which path they want to take: Happy street, or sad/mad/scared street. Explain to them that if they take sad/mad street, they will only hurt more. But, if they take happy street, they will only feel better.

Small children can begin to grasp this concept early in their lives. It is the same concept that the Buddha teaches: "Wanting is our only problem." Identities (accumulated memories) want more and more and can never be satisfied. When we 'want' from an identified place, we will get upset the instant we don't get whatever it is we want.

Wanting causes the upset (it comes from an identified place) and using the Y ends the upset.

Using the 'Y' isn't avoidance of the shadow side /identities/beliefs. It's dismissal of the idea that it has power over us. Nothing is more powerful than our own nature. The shadow side is a Jungian term used to describe unconscious parts of our personalities that we deny we have.

Wanting causes stress and taking the Y cause the disappearance of it.

Using the 'Y' is a declaration from our True Nature that it is the one in charge. It is seeing that an identity is about to overtake our lives and cause an over-reaction that will not serve us or the people around us.

My own experience of the relief of using this strategy is this: I was packing to move away from an area in which I had lived for my whole life. It didn't seem real to me that I had to move. The tears started to come within minutes of driving away.

Days before, I'd learned this valuable tool from Guy Finley.

I took the 'Y' and said "No, you don't have any authority over me," and bliss came over me. That doesn't always happen, but release always does.

Teach this to yourself and experience the wonder of it before you teach it to your child. After you've used it for a while with your child, ask them to explain it to you. Prepare to be amazed at their level of understanding.

30 Second Parenting Strategy
(a few minutes works better)
Stillness

Sometimes when we just stand still, the Grace finds us.
-Mary Davis

This strategy will change your life if you learn to sit quietly with an I-don't-know-mind, genuine curiosity, and gratitude – and ask Divine Intelligence for help with a problem.

What created you and me and the sun and the stars, has intelligence. That's why it's called Divine Intelligence or Universal Intelligence. It is ours to access any time we need to help ourselves or others (when they are under our care and not able to do this for themselves).

Creation has a 'curriculum' for us. The curriculum is for us to (un)learn and comes to us by way of upsets, as taught by Guy Finley.

When we sit in Stillness with the upset, we are able to receive the answer to the problem; the problem and the solution are only divided in our minds. We have to look inward to 'solve' our problem by 'seeing'.

One way of working with upsets, (big or small problems) is to ask this Intelligence for help. When you make sitting in Stillness into a daily ritual, even when there is no specific problem, you will become calmer, more centered, and filled with periods of peace instead of stress. Guidance happens in Stillness. Big picture, long-term, happy-making guidance is what happens when we follow where Divinity leads us. Sitting in stillness is our invitation from Divinity to 'talk' to us.

This doesn't work to win the lottery or for any negative purpose. It's to help guide you along the path that is best for you and everyone involved.

Teach this to your children after you understand it yourself.

If your child is too young to do this for themselves, you can sit quietly and ask, "What does this child need most right now?"

Today, I live my life using this valuable tool. This book came about, partly because of stillness. I sat quietly asking what it is that Creation wanted me to do.

Here is the process to get answers you need.

1. Think of a problem, close your eyes, and ask your body to be still.
2. Take comfortable breaths and follow them.
3. When the mind wanders, bring it back to stillness, but don't keep thinking about the problem. Instead, keep thinking about stillness; better yet, don't think at all.
4. Wait, with this attitude: "I know I don't know how to solve some of my problems and I'm grateful there is something more powerful and wiser than me that will help me."
5. You may get information via words, images, or you may experience a 'felt sense' immediately or at some time in the future. They are 'knowings,' different to 'thinking'. The 'knowings' are something you feel deeply, and don't feel the need to defend in any way to anyone; they just feel right. Acknowledge that you may not get an answer because you might not need to know. Or you may be asking out of selfishness rather than what's best for everyone involved and no answer will come.

I don't get answers every time. I must not need one when I don't get one.

Sometimes I do get answers and guidance (without me asking). One day I had the feeling I had to move. I didn't want to - I really, really didn't want to move again. The Universe (I'm referring to the inner wisdom, the part of us that is connected to the Universe) kept nudging me with thoughts about moving while I kept resisting them. One night, I said, okay, where do you want me to move to? I sat in Stillness for a while and then went to bed. The next morning a picture of a house was on my computer screen. I hollered out to Blake who was in the next room to come and see our new house. He said, "We're not buying a new house." I told him how I came to know we were. I knew that we would be buying that house that day. We called our realtor - it was Sunday morning at 8 am. We saw the house at 10 am and had an accepted offer by 1 pm. The inspection showed such big problems that the realtor said, "This house is a lemon, you can't buy it." I had such a strong 'knowing' that we were to live here that I told him we were buying it no matter what. Blake said to me, "I know you trust in the Universe, but are you sure?" I was so sure. I also knew one of the reasons for this move was to write my next book in this location.

These types of things have happened many times since I've given myself over to the wisdom of the Universe. Creation can't wait to guide and blossom you! Let it.

30 Second Parenting Strategy
Attitude or Gratitude?

Gratitude grows us in one direction,
attitude grows us in another.

What you 'put out there' is what you get back. This is a Universal law. It's not someone's made up fanciful idea. So, putting out genuine gratitude puts you in that desirable state more and more. Thoughts, words, and actions from a place of gratitude are simple and loving – and are completely without stress.

If your child is old enough to demand something, s/he is old enough to learn that 'gratitude' fosters joy and 'attitude' attracts misery - like a magnet.

Attitude makes demands. Demands are wants and wants are stressful. (That is different to getting what you need without a fuss).

Demands arise from expectations, which turn into emotional and mental pain because sooner or later, expectations cannot be met. If we look to the outside or the other for anything, we have to experience stress, because it is our job to give ourselves everything we truly need: compassion, patience, kindness, time, etc.

When my granddaughters start demanding something, I say, "Attitude or Gratitude?" Then I stop talking and wait.

This question is a shortcut for the teachings and questions I asked them, over many months:

"When I have attitude, it makes me grumpy. How do you feel inside when you have attitude?"

"Giving others attitude invites them to sling it back at me. It's usually instant."

"When I have gratitude, I feel good inside, and that's my goal. I don't like being crabby, I bet you don't either?"

"I love it when I feel happy inside. Gratitude does that for me. What does it do for you?"

"I don't respond to attitude, and in truth, you don't either, it feels awful inside."

"What you put out is what you get back." Invite your kids to observe their own lives, so they can prove it to themselves. One way to prove it is to smile at the people you live with all day long. Try it and see what happens. I started doing this after watching my dad do it. He would do it when he was in pain, when things didn't go his way, when he got news of ill health. He was loved tremendously by so many for doing that simple little act of brining joy to others.

"It's like the soft drink dispenser. You put two dollars in and get out two dollars-worth of the drink you choose. The same is true with attitude and gratitude. If you put attitude into the machine (life) you get the same amount of attitude (stress) out. If you put gratitude into the machine, you get the same amount of gratitude out. Which feels better to you?"

"Attitude doesn't feel good to us because it's not natural to us."

In the beginning, their lips stuck out and they stomped a bit. Now, they try not to smile and answer, "Gratitude," to my question. Their interactions change from demanding something to a gentler energy that softens their experience and stress level.

Before you give your child a device, go to the playground, or go on a fun outing, bring the child's attention to how good it feels to be grateful – about how good that feeling is. It always feels good when we think about it, before we do it. Then, when you're on your way to do the fun activity, teach them that they want to feel good after they're done, so they can remind themselves about how feeling good – feels good – even when the fun's all done! Remind them when the activity is over that we all want to feel good inside, so we are going to remember how it feels to feel good, and feel that way.

Invite yourself and your kids to notice when complaining beings. Complaining is attitude. It's also demonstrating a sense of superiority (as taught by Eckhart Tolle). If we complain, attitude grows.

For a deeper understanding of this lesson, ponder the idea that life is given freely to us (as taught by Guy Finley.) That alone, when understood, delivers the state of gratitude without any expectation whatsoever.

Many self-care experts suggest a daily gratitude ritual of some kind. Start one anytime that works for you, and above all, be genuine. Don't skip this strategy. It will change your relationship with others and with life itself. Besides, what you appreciate, appreciates (it grows), so start appreciating and watch how the Universe can't wait to *give* to you.

What you pay attention to determines your destiny, so it's never a waste of time to get in touch with gratitude.

The feeling of gratitude is a natural high. Initially it's good to be grateful for someone or something to help establish it as a practice, but eventually you'll notice that you don't need anyone or anything to experience it.

30 Second Parenting Strategy
"The Love Flooding Method"

When one loves, one does not calculate.
-Saint Therese of Lisieux

Susan Stiffleman, a parent coach for the Huffington Post, a marriage and family therapist, a credentialed teacher, and a psychotherapist is dedicated to helping parents create harmony and connection between themselves and their children. She has simple techniques to get your child to begin cooperating by increasing attachment, affinity, and love (sometimes, in a matter of minutes).

She invites you to make a list of 10 things you genuinely like about your child and then read it to them, privately.

Source:
http://parentingwithoutpowerstruggles.zreply.com/thankyou

I invite you to do this to everyone you know well enough to do it with – to create security and connection – but only when it's genuine. It creates connection and with connection, anything can be overcome.

We have had a family tradition for many years. When someone has a birthday, we each share what we genuinely like about the one celebrating the birthday. Connection.

30 Second Parenting Strategy
Saying "No"

No is a complete sentence.

There are three important but simple concepts to understand about 'no'.

One is that we often don't say no when it would be best for everyone involved if we said no. If we say yes to something we know we don't want to, we are half-hearted, ineffective, and resentful. Be honest, and, say no when that feels right.

How to kindly say no to others:

Get into your heart. Stay there. Say no. Come up with your own honest words.

— "Thank you for asking me, but I don't feel it's right for me."
— "I appreciate that you asked, but I'm unable to."
— "Thank you, but I don't feel like I can do a good job of that."
— "Thank you, my interests and commitments lie in another direction and I wish you the very best with that endeavor."
— (For charities): "Thank you, I give to another charity and really love that people like you are helping others so much."
— "Thank you for asking; I cannot take on anything else right now."

How to kindly say 'no' to your kids:

— "I'm still working out how to give you what you need and teach you what I feel is best. That's my job. I feel like what you've asked for is not the right thing right now. I'm open to talking more about this. Do you have anything you want to add to what you've told me?"

— "I feel strongly that this is not in your best interests or in ours as a family, so the answer is no. It's my job to make these decisions and I'm doing the best I can do."

— "This is a definite no. When I say this, I've taken everything that I know into consideration and feel a 'no' is best. I feel that a 'yes' would be harmful."

— "Me saying no to you doesn't mean I don't love you. It means I'm trying to do the best I can for you."

— "None of us are going to get everything we want or ask for. Right now, it doesn't work."

— "There are consequences whether I say yes or no, and I'm trying to make the best decision I can for you.

The next concept that is helpful to understand about saying no is that we sometimes jump to 'auto-no' when our kids ask for something such as an activity or something material.

Sometimes kids have great ideas and us saying no is a bad idea.

Here are some ideas that will help you kick yourself out of 'auto-no':

— Make a rule that you pause for 5 seconds and take a couple of deep breaths before you respond with an 'auto-no' to a child (except in an emergency situation, of course). Tell them you 'need a moment', as Suzi Lula teaches, and take some time. They can wait. Tell them if you can't make the decision right away.

— Ask them questions and keep yourself calm.

— Give them a chance to be heard.

— Ask more questions if you need to.

— 'Feel' into what they are saying and use that feeling to help you make a decision.
— Be honest.
— Maybe the answer is still no, but it's not a disrespectful, 'auto-no.'
— If an 'auto-no' pops out of your mouth, apologize, and say you need more information and time. Even the answer is still no, it's good to check yourself and get away from an 'auto-no.'

Another concept to understand about saying 'no', is that it does not make you a bad person, a selfish person, and/or right or wrong. As you guide your own life and that of your young child's, saying no is appropriate many times. Saying it with no charged emotions, or with less charge, feels better for everyone.

Kids push boundaries. That's how they find out where the boundaries are – so you will have to say no at times. Know that, and stay as connected to your heart as you can while doing so.

Whenever you can, say yes.

30 Second Parenting Strategy
Forgiveness

Forgiving the other is for my wellbeing, too.

Young kids automatically and quickly forgive. It's natural and less painful to us until 'wrong thinking' gets in our way.

Once they have become conditioned, kids need us to teach them how to forgive. We want the same because feeling resentful, righteous, vengeful, victimized, or hateful doesn't feel good.

When we hold a grudge, the grudge holds us.

You know how powerful forgiveness is. Once it's given, ease replaces angst. But, to give it, sometimes seems close to impossible.

Why we don't want to forgive the other:

— We think forgiving 'wrong' behavior will cause more wrong behavior.
— We think forgiving the other means they will think it's okay that they behaved that way.
— We think that we will be treated in the same awful ways if we forgive.
— We think forgiving the other doesn't right the wrong.
— We think forgiving the other makes us weak and the other, strong.
— We think forgiving the other means we're not defending ourselves, or we don't matter.

None of those are valid reasons not to forgive.

When we don't forgive, we:

— 'Live with the enemy' because they occupy our minds. My dad used to say, "I don't have an enemy. There are some people who don't like me, but I don't have any enemies." When I asked him how he did that he laughed and said, it did no good to have enemies - it didn't solve the problem.
— Stay in victimhood.
— Suffer the pain and consequences of vindictive and vengeful thoughts, words, and actions.

These strategies for forgiveness are not mainstream but are the most powerful methods I've found:

A *Course in Miracles* teaches this about forgiveness:

"What could you want that forgiveness cannot give? Do you want peace? Forgiveness offers it. Do you want happiness, a quiet mind, a certainty of purpose, and a sense of worth and beauty that transcends the world? Do you want care and safety and the warmth of sure protection always? Do you want a quietness that cannot be disturbed, a gentleness that never can be hurt, a deep, abiding comfort, and a rest so perfect it can never be upset?

All this forgiveness offers you, and more."

A *Course in Miracles* invites you to close your eyes and recall someone you don't like. "Try to perceive some light in him somewhere, a little gleam which you had never noticed. Try to find some little spark of brightness shining through the ugly picture that you hold of him. Look at this picture until you see a light somewhere within it, and, try to let this light extend until it covers him, and makes the picture beautiful and good. Look at this changed perception for a while, and, turn your mind to one you call a friend. Try to transfer the light you learned to see around your former "enemy" to him. Perceive him now as more than friend to you, for in his holiness shows you your savior, saved and saving, healed and whole. Then let him offer you the light you see in him and let your "enemy" and friend unite in blessing you with what you gave. Now [you are] one with them and they with you."

In a real-time upset, Eckhart Tolle teaches us to bring 'the light of consciousness' into an interaction or dark situation with an unconscious person, instead of labeling him or her a 'jerk'. Eckhart refers to this as non-reactivity presence, or forgiveness. This practice elevates our own level of consciousness. Do it by focussing on your breath for a moment and then asking for the 'light of consciousness' to come into this situation with the other. At this level of consciousness conflict disappears.

Guy Finley teaches that, "The true spiritual key to finding forgiveness in your heart for another is in awakening to your need to be forgiven for having been seduced into becoming someone who believes there is a valid reason for hating anyone." With your eyes closed, bring to mind your 'enemy' and ask to be forgiven for your belief that there is a valid reason for hatred.

Mooji teaches that if you see that your actions have caused pain to others, you must address it. "It is right and freeing to seek forgiveness and say ...."I'm sorry for injuring you."

"If we stay on the level of person, we cannot meet because this is where we divide. You must come to Presence and then you don't have to solve things, they dissolve by themselves."

Mooji invites us to notice this:

"Can you remember the time when you were not fighting, when you were best friends?

I don't want him to see me being happy next to him.

In conflicts we lose the power to say I'm sorry.

One of the most powerful and beautiful things you can say, is "I made a mistake, please forgive me."

Humility and courage are more powerful than the anger."

Adyashanti advises us to "Feel that unconditioned part that has no problem with humanity. That part that is all-accepting. To begin to touch upon that is to begin our humanity. It's the overwhelming acceptance. When we even touch upon it, there is a feeling of forgiveness because we are touching into that part of Being that never needs forgiveness...Compassion is selfless love."

Sit quietly and ask to 'feel that unconditional part of us, that part that doesn't judge'.

Could we have compassion for those who have hurt our identities? They are hurting, too.

Byron Katie: "We can use a lot of forgiveness. Forgiveness is about seeing that what I believed happened didn't necessarily happen. If I am thinking, putting [negative] mental post-it's on you, I am not forgiving you for being the person I believed you to be. But that's not you. So, if I take all those post its and put it on a judge your neighbor worksheet, and I question those concepts, those judgments on you, then you remain free... Now I have an enemy. I'm deluded... If I've done the work on what my mind has put on you, the next time I see you, I'm connected. I question what I believe about you and forgiveness happens. I'm the only one that can separate me from another human being. If I'm not connected, that's on me. I look at what I'm thinking and do The Work on it. If I've done anything to hurt you out of that unkind mind, I admit it and I apologize and all the bread crumbs [posties]that appear are gone. It's quite a turnaround for the ego. If it's not sincere, I wouldn't do it, so I wait until I am. I make it right where I can. If I've gossiped about you, influenced someone negatively about you, I need to go back to those people and say, I was nuts and I would say this man is a kind man, a good man, I'd be telling the truth because I've really done my work. If I want to be right, that's my first clue, there is an attachment there, it's time for me to identify what I'm thinking about this other human being, those judgments, and assumptions. This is the only way I know to see them as they really are. We are talking about complete forgiveness, total forgiveness." www. thework.com

Do a version of Ho'oponopono on these ideas in relation to your 'enemy', feeling the feelings each statement brings up:

— I'm so sorry I'm identified with betrayal. Please forgive me. Thank you. I love you.
— I'm sorry I'm identified with grudges. Please forgive me. Thank you. I love you.
— I'm sorry I'm identified with harming others and being harmed. Please forgive me. Thank you. I love you.
— I'm sorry I'm identified with regret. Please forgive me. Thank you. I love you.
— I'm sorry I'm identified with vengeance, getting even and retribution. Please forgive me. Thank you. I love you.
— I'm sorry I'm identified with hatred. Please forgive me. Thank you. I love you.

Find the cause of the other's 'betrayal'. Sit quietly and ask what you gained from the other treating you the way they did that hurt you? You may get answers like: I was the 'good' one, I was right, I am a decent person. Wait until you get a positive word. You will feel it when it's the right word for you. That will explain why you (unconsciously) wanted them to betray you in the first place. This does not make their behavior appropriate; it just sets you free of a belief that causes betrayal in the first place. I'm sorry if this seems harsh – I'm making it sound like we are beacons for hurt and betrayal. We are, based on our beliefs, and by doing this work we change our operating system and become beacons for love.

30 Second Parenting Strategy
Power Struggles

True power is peaceful.
True peace is powerful.

Children feel powerless at times – simply recall your own childhood to get in touch with that.

We think toddlers and small children don't know what's best for them, and in most cases we're right. Toddlers can't decide for themselves when to go to bed, when to have a bath, or if it's safe to cross the street; they need guidance. It's a parent's job to decide FOR the child until the natural process of gaining maturity happens. However, falling into the old pattern of power plays with a toddler or teenager hasn't solved any problems.

Even though children never get everything they want, they don't stop trying. The persistence they can demonstrate would almost be admirable if it wasn't so stressful to their parents.

To meet this dilemma with some understanding, it is helpful to look into our own lives and behaviors.

If one person is attempting to control something or someone, and the other doesn't engage, the one initiating the power play loses the power.

Also, it's not rational to use reason with someone who is in the middle of a power play. Reason can't compete with an identity that's irrational. All identities are irrational.

Also, we sometimes try to use our own special brand of 'reason' that's really just a power play. Using reason this way can look like, 'I'm right and you're wrong'. That's not reason. It's a proclamation.

Reflect on this:

Is there a need to change them? Are you wanting someone to be perfect? Could you be okay with them doing what they are doing? Look at the ways you are causing yourself stress with wanting the other to change. When there are time restraints, you can mention them, and let everyone do what they are doing. Notice you don't really need power in those moments - and use the time to practice these strategies instead of making a power play.

Power plays have consequences and don't deliver power anyway.

So, the question is, will power really give us freedom from the entrapment we felt as children and feel as adults? No.

The bottom line is the more secure you feel inside of yourself, the less power struggles you will have with your children and others.

True security arrives as a blessing when you begin to see that life is completely out of your hands (Sadhguru). It's a simple truth that we can't control (some of) what comes at in in life.

How you respond to it is completely in your hands. (Sadhguru)

Each time you do self-inquiry, you come closer to your own Nature and our Nature doesn't need power. It *is* power.

In the meantime, what can you do about your power struggle issues? Begin to recognize when you feel you need to control the child (or another.) That's enough to begin to change it. It seems hard to tell the truth and admit that you are in a power struggle with anyone, never mind a two-foot-tall child – but we often are.

Ask yourself if what you really want is power. Ask yourself if you need to control another person. Ask yourself what you hope to gain by having power over another. Ask why you need power. Ask yourself if there is another way, and see what bubbles up. It's all about asking questions that you don't ordinarily ask.

Notice that you are all stirred up and in a power struggle with a tiny child. Sit down. Breathe. Put the problem with the child on paper in a clear sentence. Ask yourself questions about the problem. Wait and see what comes up. Use your favorite strategy and return to calmness.

When you give yourself this kind of power, you end struggle.

30 Second Parenting Strategy
The Stages of Conflict

Speak when you are angry and
you will make the best speech you will ever regret.
-Groucho Marx

Dr. Shefali explains that every conflict has 3 stages: lack, anxiety, and seeking control.

Source:
Dr. Shefali: The Conscious Parent https://www.pinterest.com/pin/377 035800026822798/

We are talking mainly about the kind of lack/unmet needs like freedom, respect, love, compassion, sovereignty over our own lives, kindness, connection, peace, solitude, to hear ourselves, etc.

Unmet needs/lack can also be more basic, like food, clothing, shelter, water.

If we feel lack, we will experience anxiety and seek control over others or situations.

Upsets come from 'identifying' with whatever we lack.

If we feel we lack love, our behavior will be that of an unloved person: cold, short, demanding, selfish, rebellious, tense, aggravating, defiant, small, self-righteous, etc.

If you pay close attention to yourself during an upset, you will notice that:

1. You want something (there is lack but you don't really know what it's about yet).
2. You feel upset or anxiousness.
3. You want to control the situation or the other to get what you want.

Most often, we don't know what our real need is in an upset. You will have to get used to looking 'under' what you think you want. By doing this you find the real problem, and, the solution is to give whatever you lack – to yourself.

For example, you might get upset or feel conflicted when people cut you off in traffic. What we think we want is for others to be safe drivers. We are lacking the feeling of safety, so anxiety appears. We want control of the other in that moment and we want them to do what we want. There is no way to change the other, but there is a way to give ourselves what we need. In this case, it's good to remind ourselves that nothing bad has happened (we are safe, on the road and alive). To feel in control, we can bring our full attention to the act of driving, to the proximity of other vehicles, etc.

When your child acts out with upsetting behaviors, sit quietly, and ask yourself, "What is lacking? What does this child really need? Can I provide it? Can they provide if for themselves?"

For example, if a child is screaming in the grocery store, the stages they will go through are: they think they have lacked something, they are having an emotional response, and are trying to control you by screaming or having a fit. Reminding yourself of these stages can help you keep calmer.

If it's an unconscious adult that's acting out, the best you can do is get present and stay that way; don't be dragged along into unconsciousness. Notice the stages they go through. Focus on your breath, which takes you out of thinking and back into yourself where Presence is possible.

30 Second Parenting Strategy
Negativity in a Young Child

Guy Finley teaches "The importance of never meeting a child's negative state on the same level of negativity. To truly help a child who is negative we must observe what that behavior elicits in us and meet it with awareness."

This means we need to notice ourselves when our child is negative and see what we are accusing the child of. That will move us out of our own negativity, and take us as a Present parent to the interaction.

The 30 Second Parenting Strategy called 'I Am That' shows us how to do this. When we take our attention inwards, it often changes the energy of others because we no longer have a 'hook' that can keep conflict alive.

Source:
http://www.guyfinley.org/free-content/video/4977

A New Perspective on Bullies
Dr. Shefali and Eckhart Tolle Speak on Bullying

Putting out the other's light
will not make our own shine brighter.

-Unknown

Dr. Shefali invites us to consider that "Bullies, having learned that they are 'bad' or 'not good enough,' and attempt to rid themselves of this message by projecting the same message onto a child who is 'slightly off center,' 'not good enough', and chooses that child/person as their victim."

She teaches that the victim unknowingly 'accepts' the bullying because they too, believe they are not good enough.

Children live what they learn.

Video: 5:54
https://www.youtube.com/watch?v=uQOcBvJ4kXs

30 Second Parenting Strategy
How to Stop Bullying

All bullies suffer from insecurity.
All victims suffer from insecurity.

This insightful teaching awareness comes from Eckhart Tolle and Dr. Shefali.

The cure for bullies and their victims is to help them find security.

If your child is being bullied, find ways to make them feel secure:

— Teach them the methods that create connection: Diverting to Divinity (30 Second Parenting Strategy).
— Do the 'Love Flooding' method to help them feel secure.
— Read them/give them Milton's Secret by Eckhart Tolle. Milton's Secret shows the true resolution lies on the inner level.
— From age 7 up to adult, teach them inner work (these strategies) so they can clear the energy patterns within them that attract bullies.
— Make sure they understand that they must tell an adult they trust no matter what the bully has said.

If your child is the bully: do the above with the child, and rather than making sure they tell an adult, tell them the consequences of harming another person:

— It could become a matter for the school authorities.
— The police could become involved.

— They don't feel good inside when they bully, and they do feel good inside when they care for others.
— Assure them that they are not 'bad' but they are responsible for their behavior.
— Help them see that it's so much more natural to be kind, and, that kindness has much different consequences.

The interactive course, "Bully Proof Yourself (And Your Kids)" will set you free from bullying (whether you are a bully or being bullied). It's found on www.courserebel.com under Brenda Miller.

It's (My) Right to Blame Another! Or Is It?

Blaming is a lost opportunity for peace.

It's important to express and it's as important not to harm others while doing it.

There is a modern perception that everyone needs to be heard. **While that's very true, it's truer that the truth needs to be heard and blaming isn't it. So, if expressing our upsets includes hurting or blaming the other, we don't have that right.**

Blaming will make things worse, not better. It's important to begin to notice blaming for what it is so we can be set free of stress it causes.

Without knowing anything about blaming, it's easy enough to see that we feel uncomfortable inside when we blame. That's enough to let us know that something is out of alignment.

Blaming is a mistake we make that keeps us in the painful cycle of 'being right' instead of just Being.

We think blaming is how to alleviate our own inner pain, and keep ourselves innocent and safe. We use blaming to make ourselves look good, but someone who blames never looks good. That could be enough for us to consider that blaming isn't achieving the desired results.

Blaming can't solve a problem.

When we blame the other; say they are responsible for how we feel inside, then we have no power or sovereignty over our own inner states; we're saying others do, and are unknowingly agreeing to be powerless.

Powerlessness is a carry-over thought from experiencing and then attaching to the idea of powerlessness as children. It's not meant to be a life-long companion.

We're looking for some kind of power, but the kind of power we feel when we've blamed another isn't true power.

Power isn't real or useful unless it's peaceful.

Power that is violent or manipulative is tyranny or dictatorship.

Ghandi demonstrated the power of peace when they were trying to take back control of India. When they came to arrest him, Ghandi said he wasn't going to go with them and invited them to have tea with him. They sat and had tea. Those who occupied India didn't know what to do with that kind of peace. Peace changes the whole dynamic of the interaction. Always.

True peace is true power.

If we believe the other has power over us and makes us feel the way we do, then we are also agreeing that the other is who will make us feel in other ways like happy, fulfilled, and loved.

The problem with that is that the other and anything in the outer world are not capable of giving us any naturally, long-lasting happy states (think of your partner, that new car, house, pair of shoes – they can't provide long-term, unshakable joy). Everyone has noticed that by now; maybe we haven't given it much thought, but it's clear that unshakable happiness and peace can't be provided by anyone else or anything else. Where does it come from then?

It's built into us and currently obscured by our own beliefs.

Simple logic: Other people, situations, events; none of those things can cause the long-term inner state of joyfulness. In the same way, they cannot cause our upset state, either.

It's so pivotal to understand this. **Joy IS an inside job. If we understand this, we take full control over all of own inner states, and, transforming upsets to peace becomes the useful norm.**

We blame because it's how we've always done it. If blame doesn't work, let's not do it anymore. Or, when we catch ourselves doing it, let's at least retract the blame, apologize, and see what's truly going on inside of us that needs attention.

We don't have to do something because it's always been done that way. I remember hearing a story about a woman who always cut the end off of her ham before she cooked it but didn't know why, other than her grandmother and mother did it. When she asked her grandmother why she did it, her grandmother told her that the ham was always too big for the pan and that's why she cut the end of it off. It works the same with beliefs: we see it done and do it without questioning it.

That's how we operate: if it's taught, passed down, always done that way, it must be right, and we do it thinking it's the right way to live.

If whatever we do works, brings peace and harmony to all, then it's okay, it's dharmic; it's the right thing to do; anything less than that is beneath us.

Blaming IS beneath us. As the Buddha taught, harming another is also beneath us and blaming the other harms them.

Blaming only happens when we are operating outside of the pure intelligence we are born with.

This book will reconnect you with your own inner intelligence and blaming and hurting will no longer be a part of expressing ourselves.

This doesn't happen overnight – unless it does.

Creation has a plan for us to express ourselves creatively and in service to all of life. Those kinds of expressions are natural and worthy of each of us.

We make so many more problems for ourselves if we don't see the truth of living this way.

When we do the work in this book, the focus is on solutions, not problems. Eventually one doesn't live from a problem/solution viewpoint, but from a place of gratitude for whatever happens. There are a few steps in between, though!

When you employ these simple tools, you will find that you naturally speak to children differently and still communicate what you need. The need for blame and punishment disappears into conversation, discovery, respect, curiosity, and most important of all: true good will towards all. It's a beautiful and natural high.

We were meant to blossom, not blame. The more we blame, the less we blossom.

(Psychological) Stress Is Not Normal

If stress burned calories, I'd be a supermodel.
-Many claim to have said this.

Stress is so familiar we've begun to think it's a normal part of life that we have to live with. It's another mistake we make as human beings to believe that.

Stress is stressful, it's not normal, as taught by Sadhguru, and experienced by each of us!

Using negativity (which always feel stressful) as a tool to get kids to comply doesn't work because it doesn't connect us. We think that dominating them with anger or disapproving of them gets us what we want, but it *really* just disconnects us and causes more stress.

Choose This:

It's simply amazing to watch the upset in a child (or in ourselves) disappear and see naturalness take over.

Or Choose This:

If we don't do inner work during or after an upset, the negative energy becomes harmful words and actions and makes the situation worse.

Every single pointer in this book will reduce stress and deflate those big, uncontrollable emotions we wish we didn't have.

Stress is not part of our nature unless we're running out of the way of an oncoming vehicle.

It's created by us.

While it's true that stress is not normal, stress is pretty familiar. It's also true that stress damages our relationships, our minds, and our bodies. Stress is destructive and we can't be here just to self-destruct and destroy the spirit in others.

There is more proof that stress is not normal: when you use the strategies in this book and begin to 'rest in peace' (*while you're alive*), it's easy to see that child-like states infused with calmness and wisdom are normal and come naturally to us. After a while, it's obvious that stress is not normal.

Stress makes us feel and act crazy.

It's not normal to feel crazy, it's crazy to feel crazy.

It's not normal to feel frustrated, it's just frustrating.

It's not normal to feel angry, scared, sad, or worried. It's painful to feel those ways.

Stress is a sign that we are out of alignment with Creation. It's a call for help. These strategies are help.

You are the only one who can give yourself long-term relief from stress. The reason for that is because what you need to find is inside of you. Nobody can do that for you. Others can offer pointers to peace, but only you can find what they point to.

As hard as it is to believe, from our current understanding, there *are* people on the planet who live without stress. They have gone before us, and from shores that seem distant to our own, have left their messages for us to discover – messages that will help us find our way. The secrets they possess are what each of us possess but have been obscured from our own awareness.

Without knowing we did it, we covered up secrets about life that we hold inside of us with learned ideas that aren't based on how life works.

Every single pointer in this book will open up natural and joyful states of wellbeing that pre-exist inside of us. This is provable only by you using the strategies and experiencing it for yourself.

One huge benefit as you work with each strategy is that you will stop thinking you need to know everything. There is a lot of pressure on parents to know what they're doing and that's stressful. You will give yourself a big break when you make mistakes; every mistake you've made with your child has been out of love and concern for them. Also, there is a little-known secret available for all of us: you'll realize that you can call on Divine Intelligence any time you want – It's open for customer service 24/7 and each of us are its customers. No exceptions.

And don't forget Blessing Mistakes!

Have you heard of Divine Intervention? Divine Intelligence is kind of like that only we can take the initiative and ask for help with any issue we have. If that seems far-fetched to you, doesn't it make sense that if we are to blossom and shine as human beings, that there must some guidance somewhere? It makes sense to me that whatever created us didn't drop us here and then leave us to fend for ourselves.

When you tap into Universal Intelligence, life takes a U-turn into effortlessness, acceptance, and clarity. That's connection at its best. It also relieves us of having to 'know' everything. Going into Stillness to ask questions, as a parent, is one of the strategies you will learn in this book. It's also a way out of any stressful situation.

I have been prone to feeling a lot of stress when I think about or am around addicts. When I sit in stillness (sit quietly with no distractions) and ask what to do, I get very clear messages. One of them is, "Tell them you love them." The 'fixer' in me, and the 'one who disapproves' in me, disappears and love speaks for me.

The stress I feel is not normal, it's just familiar, both because I've been around people experiencing addiction and have experienced addictions myself, my whole life.

I imagine, when I talk to them, they would rather hear that I love them than my opinion on addiction and what they 'should' do. I don't even know what to do many times. My disapproval isn't for me to share with them. My disapproval is mine to work out and not put on anyone else. I'm quite sure that whatever created me didn't put me here to disapprove or judge any other human being.

The conversation that holds any type of disapproval or negativity spirals downwards quickly. The conversation that holds love connects and uplifts us in ways nothing else can.

I don't know what it is an addict must experience in order to come into awareness of their beautiful nature. It must be addiction because that's what they are/I am experiencing. I've gained so many awarenesses about addiction by sitting still and asking to be shown what I need to, to bring myself into understanding.

Wisdom is waiting for us if we just get quiet and ask. Thinking we know usually gets us in trouble.

As you go through the book, you will begin to see that your child is a unique possibility – not a stress-inducing little person, not someone sent here for you to control. No one else is like them, or you, or me. Once you understand this, you can figure out ways for both them and you to blossom. It's a tremendous relief when that becomes the focus instead of stressful problems or flaws.

Having said all that – given you those plums - this work is not for the faint of heart. It's humbling and challenging. It asks you to try a new strategy the next time there is a stressful upset, and if you do, you will see from a new and more peaceful place. It also invites you to switch the focus from stressful surface skirmishes to the 'deep' (stillness) where you will find wellbeing for yourself and your child.

Every mom/dad wants to go from these stressful states:

> 'feeling guilty'
> 'feeling angry'
> 'feeling confused'
> 'feeling exhausted'
> 'feeling reactive'
> 'feeling ashamed'
> 'feeling punishing'
> 'feeling resentful'

> to these natural states:

> 'joyful"
> 'calm'
> 'energized'

'compassionate'
'genuine'
'supportive'

I wanted to be a great parent, but I was an asleep and stressed-out parent. I hope this book helps you avoid some of the painful experiences that unconscious parenting resulted in for me and, by extension, for my children and grandchildren. We pass down so much more than our hair color and eye color to our children. We pass down ways of living that don't work, like hollering, demanding, punishing, controlling, and arguing. When we do that to our kids, they grow up and do the same and that's not what we want for them. If it's true that's not what we want for them, then we have to stop modelling that.

Just to be clear: stress is not natural and it's not normal. It's stressful.

Perfection

No one is perfect, that's why pencils have erasers.
-A popular saying – by many.

We secretly want a perfect child based on our own imperfect *ideas of a* perfect child. Always polite, yet not a pushover; extremely intelligent - to the point of being gifted – yet truly humble; competent, neat, clean, funny, helpful, respectful, etc. etc. etc. This type of perfect human being doesn't exist and yet we continually make the mistake of wanting it.

Simple Logic: Continuing to want what doesn't exist *makes no sense.*

We want perfection and, instead, get our projection. Every time a child acts out, if we get upset about it, it's because we've got some of that same thing in us and, of course, we don't like it. The reason we don't like it is that it's out of line with who we really are.

The paradox is that perfection appears when we are deeply connected.

Take the idea of perfection out with the trash!

Punishment

Punishment cannot heal spirits, can only break them.
-Barbara Deming

There isn't a parent in the world who hasn't punished their child, felt that they were right to do it, and then felt awful for doing it.

If we're right when we punish, why would we feel awful (guilty or upset) for doing it?

Simple logic: If we don't feel peaceful over our actions, they're not peaceful and will cause ourselves and others pain.

It seems like there isn't another way other than to punish your child (and yourself) until you begin to carefully and HONESTLY EXAMINE PUNISHMENT AS IT IS, NOT AS WE BELIEVE IT TO BE.

Punishment is aggression so that's what it teaches. It also teaches submission, and disconnection which brings up fear and terror.

For now, when you find punishment is your 'go to' just notice that you don't know another way and have as much compassion for yourself as you can. You can do that by using Blessing Mistakes on yourself, "I matter so much more than the mistake I've made of punishing (myself or another person)."

Then use one of the other tools from this book or elsewhere to find out the truth of the cause of the upset (the upset that would make you punish a child).

Punishing anyone never gets the desired results.

Notice that punishing a child doesn't cause connection, it causes a child to grow up and punish themselves and others. Notice that nobody feels good when punishment happens. Noticing is enough to begin to change how you feel and function in your life.

Noticing comes from a higher level of consciousness which is why it causes transformation.

We don't know another way, *yet*. We know punishing is a mistake, intuitively. Our hearts don't condone punishment because it's not part of our Nature to punish. It's our Nature to guide and provide.

When to Correct A Child

In a gentle way, you can shake the world.
-Mahatma Gandhi

A true correction directed at a child has no negatively charged energy in it and comes from our genuine concern for how they feel inside.

A false correction has a negative charge and is given in an attempt to:

— Change the child.
— Bring us peace and quiet.
— Temporarily release our own stress by taking out our moods on a child.
— Make a child materially successful as a replacement for inner joy.

False corrections live inside of us, and if we do this work, they die inside of us and our child's wellbeing (inner state) becomes our focus.

When a child does or says something and we feel upset, that's our cue to do our own work before we offer them a correction. That will not always be possible in the upsetting moment while we are transitioning from operating through our lower dual nature to our higher nature, so it's good enough to do the work after the upset.

Over-reactions (upsets) that come from identities can be so strong sometimes, that the reaction happens without conscious thought. In plain language, sometimes we holler, scold, and otherwise correct a child because we are too identified (overtaken by a false belief) that we can't do anything other than act from that place. When that happens, don't berate yourself, and don't let it slip by because upsets accumulate in the system and come back to get our attention until we 'get' our lesson.

Bless your mistake (give yourself Grace, not grief when you make the mistake of punishing a child rather than gently correcting them) by saying to yourself, "I matter more than the mistake." Then make the mistake right by apologizing to the child.

Do your own inner work to expose the identities, which allows you to clearly see what correction the child really needs.

For a correction to be honest and effective it is naturally done without disapproval, condemnation, or punishment. If we feel any negativity while correcting the child, we are doing it from an identified place and it's not an effective correction.

A true correction comes without judgment; the adult offers the correction from the wisdom of, and being anchored in their own True Nature. They want the child to have what they want: freedom from stress.

A valuable and proper correction is always aimed at dissolving an identity in ourselves or the child. That's what inner work does. Dissolving identities is the point; not 'teaching'. That leaves the child operating from their natural self which doesn't need teaching; it's True Nature already knows. Teaching has an important role in our society, obviously – but you can't 'teach' True Nature.

If we become observers of ourselves, it will become clear to us that if we adopt ways of living in the world that don't serve us or the other, we suffer. If we behave meanly, rudely or in any other negative way towards another, in the moments we are behaving in those ways we don't feel good. That's because we're out of our True Nature and into our learned, conditioned, lower nature. Most of the time we skip over how we are feeling inside and focus on letting the other have a piece of our mind. That moment of feeling upset inside HOLDS the key to transforming upsets into peace. It IS the message about what we are falsely identifying with/connecting to in the moment. This book holds many strategies to uncover and dissolve beliefs that cause pain.

The possibility of pain or peace in the upset moment (or after the upset has happened) is the same for all human beings. What we do with the upset determines our inner state. If we do inner work, the problems dissolve and if we don't, they reincarnate. You can prove this to yourself with this work.

Remember that children, without knowing it, are teaching us what they want us to teach them: they want connection with their True Nature. That understanding (that they have a True Nature that has no stress) will serve them well when they are faced with the inevitable challenges we are all faced with. It falls upon us to teach them this inner work as the primary corrective tool because that's what will bring them (and all humans) back into peace.

Life is Urging Us Towards Wholeness

If the whole world followed you,
would you be pleased with where you took it?
                                    -Neale Donald Walsch

Our current focus isn't on our wholeness. It's on division, it's on good and bad, it's on pain and pleasure. What if we focused on what's going on inside of us, what's in our hearts? Not from an 'I should' place, but from a place of soft, inner knowing.

Don't you want to know if that place is possible for you? I sure did.

I became a student of life and of whomever or whatever was in front of me. I wanted to find wholeness. At first that seemed like, at best, empty words, and at worst, whimsical. I wanted to see if there was another way to live life and relate to others, *especially kids.*

I find it so ironic that it was kids who started to teach me about wholeness.

One of the many amazing lessons I received from a child happened when I was sitting on the deck one summer day with my foot dangling in the kiddie pool. My 18-month-old granddaughter was happily splashing about when she stood up, gave me the most beautiful smile, then bent over and watched herself pee in the pool. She looked up and said, "Pee, Grama!" and beamed at me. For an unknown reason, I instantly understood that there was a lesson available to me, one that she already 'knew'. I stayed silent for a moment to be shown the lesson. It was that peeing was blissful and she didn't want me to focus on the idea that peeing in the pool was 'bad', even if that's not where pee efficiently goes. Peeing and all other body functions are wonderful, and we need to teach them that at the same time we teach them that pee goes in the potty. Instead, we teach them duality: good and bad. You're good if you go on the potty and bad if you go in the pool. What if neither are true? What if that's not the focus?

What if the focus is: pee does go in the potty AND it feels so wonderful to pee? Is there anything else to be taught about potty training? Kids are going to pee in places we wish they wouldn't, that's just a fact. They are not going to have the required cognitive function and bladder control until they do.

Why have we made that and everything else into good and bad? When we divide life into good and bad – good and bad become inevitable, and worse, become the lens we experience life through.

When we teach children simple truths, they will naturally and peacefully co-exist in the world.

We taught our granddaughter the lesson that she taught us: bodily functions are fantastic (and some of them go in the potty). We didn't teach good and bad. She potty trained herself. No stress. She taught me wholeness by teaching me the part I was missing when I was teaching her: peeing feels natural and absolutely great. It's not a nuisance to have to pee. It's a pleasure. Don't forget that! A peeing accident is easily fixable. It's easier to clean up a mess than undo a belief system.

By observing children, I've learned that they want us to help keep them connected to their True Nature: they want to be natural. What's natural is that pee goes on the potty unless it didn't and then it's natural to clean it up with love as the guide. Peace wants to shine through every action we take.

Life's Lessons

Find the lesson, forget the pain.

It's important to remember that life's lessons or challenges don't stop. They don't stop because we want them to stop, they don't stop because we feel like we've had enough, they don't stop because we've 'done lots of consciousness work', they don't stop because we're good people; they don't stop BECAUSE evolution IS the process. The way Creation works is that it sends us a lesson via an upset when we're out of sync with Universal laws. If we use the upset, we will come back into sync and feel peaceful. In that way, we evolve. If we don't, we get another lesson. Creation loves us so much that the lesson will be taught repeatedly with more strength until we get it. Creation is on our side; it wants us to wake up and shine.

What if we could understand that every awful thing we've ever said or done happened because we were being unknowingly guided by our 'human programmed compass', not our 'Human Being Compass'? What if we could understand that our upsetting thoughts, words, and actions could be no other way because unconsciousness is our (unknown) inner guide?

A deep understanding of this brings a paradox to life: forgiveness is unnecessary if the ways we've acted could be no other way, and, at the same time, forgiveness frees us. BUT that's not the point of this strategy.

The real point is: what is my 'Human Being Compass' and how do I uncover that in me? Where is that guide in us? Can we find it?

It is the most important thing we can ever do as human beings.

Our kids are going to learn how to dot an 'i', cross a 't', and count to one hundred and beyond. Their inborn intelligence exceeds those basics by far; so, while that needs some attention, don't focus so much on that. If the focus is on their True Nature and helping them stay connected or get reconnected to that, everything else will fall into place.

If they are connected, they will know firsthand that they have a natural place of peace inside of them, and that will keep them sane in a world filled with people who aren't. Are they going to experience the Human Being Compass and follow their hearts? Or are they going to experience the human programmed compass and follow their heads? Are they going to feel the grandness (as Byron Katie says) of "Joy for no reason" – and live from that place? Isn't that what we really want for our children? And for ourselves? There is nothing wrong with a college education unless we don't have joy as our constant companion; otherwise, that education will cause so much stress, we'll wish we could run away, and might. Or, we'll get physically sick from all the stress. Or we'll live in the unnatural state of experiencing negativity rather than experiencing the peaceful aliveness of life.

It is my wish that this kind of information be taught in schools so that learning about the inner world is at least as important as learning about the outer world.

Our True Nature

Rediscover your belly laugh!

Our True Nature is what genuinely feels natural. This state comes from the Being part of us. There is never discomfort present when we are in our True Nature.

Our lower nature or ego is what feels unnatural, uncomfortable, uneasy, unintelligent, ungrateful, unforgiving, unaccepting, and unworthy. These states come from false ideas we've learned.

The Being part of the human has largely been ignored, with all the attention given to the human aspects.

What if who, how, and what we are is really this: joyful without cause, unendingly grateful, naturally playful, authentic, compassionate, and filled with a kind of love that has no single direction or prejudice. What if that's who we are? What do thoughts, words and actions look like from that place?

There is proof that is who we are. When we are in any of those states that come naturally to us, we FEEL natural.

More proof: when we act out, or experience upset, we never feel natural; we feel unnatural with anything from a hardly detectible sense of unease all the way to full, blown over-reactiveness. Neither of those upset states, or any state in between feels natural to us. If you pay close attention to how you feel when you are upset or how you feel when you are behaving poorly, you will also notice that you don't feel natural; you feel discomfort. That's proof that upsets are unnatural. When we are coming from an unnatural place, that's how we feel. When we're natural, we don't feel discomfort.

At the same time, upsets are unavoidable because they are exactly what grow us up and out of our human programming into our Human Being.

Upsets are the sign that we need to see what we're believing that isn't true so that we can come back into our True Selves and when we do, we experience relief.

If peaceful and joyful is who we are, then "Who is this other one?" (as Mooji asks), who keeps showing up to holler, boil over, feel frustrated and impatient. Who is this one who keeps appearing to say and do mean things, argue, fight, be captured and held hostage by emotions that act out all of the things we wish we wouldn't?

Who is that one?

That's our 'learned' or 'conditioned' selves; the 'human programmed compass'. We learned we'd get something we thought we wanted by speaking and behaving in those ways. We might think we get what we want, but unless we're getting "Joy for no reason," (as Byron Katie says), we're not getting what we really want.

We've all seen little kids misbehaving (burping loudly on purpose, hitting their siblings, etc.), and an adult laughing happily at them and saying how cute they are. From that, the child learns that misbehaving gets approval and is cute. Then, it becomes a belief (an idea, an identity, a formula) that operates us: acting out gets us approval and it's cute. See the insanity?

This is how beliefs are formed, and then repeated - unless we plan our own intervention. The work you do here is your own intervention.

Neither the parents nor the children are aware of what is being taught and learned. The parents learned it from their parents, and so on. Blame would be pointless; this goes back too many generations.

We humans have been instilling beliefs instead of uncovering truths for a very long time.

What we learned is not who we are. A belief can't be who we are. Who we are can't be 'cute if we are acting out'. Yet we learn to believe that acting out makes us cute. It's not cute at all as we get older. It's just acting out with consequences nobody likes.

It's normal to come into the world, learn the wrong stuff, and transmute it into the right stuff. An understanding of that makes us grateful for all of our experiences. It also teaches us not to judge; every one of us is going through the same process.

Awareness is The Secret

*Every time you are tempted to react in the same
old way, ask yourself if you want to be a prisoner
of the past or a pioneer of the future.*
                                                -Deepak Chopra

It's time to clearly recognize that most everything we've ever tried has not caused permanent, positive change in our lives. In fact, anything outside of consciousness work, (or anything other than becoming aware), has not caused the transformation we desperately long for, especially as it relates to how we interact with our children.

Wanting things to be different won't actually make change happen.

Awareness is what makes change deep and lasting. How we know this to be true is that any 'aha' moment (which is awareness) stops us and makes us ponder. Because an 'aha' comes from truth, an illusion can't continue to exist once it's been exposed (like 'it's cute to act out'). Awareness dissolves beliefs. Awareness comes from a higher level of consciousness inside of us than the mind is working at (when it is in belief-mode). A belief can't produce an 'aha' higher than itself. Belief's produce "I know," and then defense. Awareness IS Beingness giving us information from a higher level that will help us up to that same higher level. It's our Human Being Compass.

If we have an 'aha' moment, it changes how we perceive, which changes how we think, and then how we feel, speak, and act.

An awareness of the stillness in a tree, the vastness of the sky, the majesty of the mountains - doesn't come from the level of the mind that believes. The mind can't even compute that kind of immenseness.

When we have an awareness, or an 'aha' moment, nobody could tell us it isn't true. We have a deep feeling connected with the awareness that is solid. We don't feel the need to defend it, argue about it, or even tell another person unless it serves to. It comes with a stillness about it, and it doesn't require explanation; it just is.

Wise men and women, sages, saints, and shamans know this. We can too!

The level we perceive at is what determines our experience of life.

Our awareness determines what we perceive.

Awareness changes what we perceive.

When sailors thought the world was flat, they worried about falling off of it and didn't want to go far because of that. Their loved ones sat at home worrying and fearful about them falling off of the end of the world. When the awareness happened that the world was round, it changed how far sailors would go, and it lifted the worry and fear of falling off of the planet. While this is an example of awareness changing us in the physical/outer world, it's used here because it's easy to see how important awareness is and how our level of awareness will determine what we perceive, and therefore, our experience of life.

An example of inner awareness is this: we believe an 'I'dea that a vacation, a different partner, a new job, a new home, food, etc. will give us pleasure so we focus on getting that, believing that's the answer. If we question that, or bring our attention to that idea to see if it's true or not, we will begin to bring awareness to it. While there is nothing wrong with those things used intelligently, we will begin to see that none of those things cause long-term pleasure and that new awareness is what allows us to move our attention to what will bring us long-term pleasure. If we really see that these things are not the answer, see that they are not taking us to 'The Promised Land', then that awareness will change us.

Each of these strategies brings us into awareness.

Awareness is THE *peacemaker* BECAUSE IT COMES FROM OUR TRUE NATURE, FROM CREATION, FROM UNIVERSAL INTELLIGENCE. It comes from a higher level than mind can operate at.

We are receptors for that intelligence. As Eckhart teaches, we are seeds for consciousness. The person or personality doesn't wake up, come into consciousness, it can't. Consciousness can sprout through us, though, and peace is what happens when it does.

All 'aha's' feel peaceful because they are truth.

As Guy Finley teaches, a good prayer repeated as often as possible during the day is, "More of Thee, Less of Me." That means please fill me with Universal Intelligence and less of my own beliefs and unintelligence. One I like is, "Divine Intelligence, do with me what YOU will."

Deep inside, we know teaching kids the nonsense we lived by (that didn't work) isn't going to make them happy, healthy, or successful. Yet, we continue to teach them only because we don't know a different way.

There is a different way.

Why are We All Such A Mess?

"Illusion is the first pleasure."

Osho

For most of our lives, we have, unknowingly, put our attention on the wrong things hoping to gain happiness, success, and wellbeing.

Sadhguru teaches that if we were naturally free as a child, (and we were, for most of it, no matter how bad things got in some moments) as we grow, shouldn't we become freer, or at least maintain that same amount of carefree abandon we experienced as children? Why do we regress into these negative states that don't serve anyone or anything? We are attached to illusions and looking for illusions to give us pleasure.

Even if we remember some traumas, the truth is that each of those specific traumas took a minute or two (as taught by many Masters, and by sitting down and looking at any trauma I've ever experienced). Sometimes the traumas happened quite a few times, but the rest of the time that we don't remember, we were just being ourselves with no need to remember anything. Trauma's take a few minutes and yet we carry them, sometimes, for a lifetime.

Why? Because we let them define us and don't even know we're doing it. Then we unconsciously gain a sense of 'self' from the trauma; who I am is the one who _____ (you fill in the blank with a traumatic situation that happened in your life).

In an unintentional and odd way, we begin to take pleasure in the trauma. You can see this is true by how much pleasure we get in telling the tale of the trauma over and over and over. The pleasure we get isn't real pleasure.

We are looking to the wrong things (house, car, job, kids, money, health, etc.) to make us feel whole, fulfilled, happy, we're living in an illusion. They can't bring permanent internal happiness to us. An illusion can't create true, lasting pleasure.

Does the mirage of an oasis have any water?

Does it make sense to you that we are only a physical being? If that's true, then why do we have 'spiritual' experiences? Why do we feel so remarkable when we gaze into the night sky? Why do we forget ourselves when the other is in real need? Might there be something other than 'I' that could operate us?

Joseph Campbell, discovered through mythology that there is something unseen that gives rise to the seen, and that's it more powerful than what is seen. Every Master I've studied says this outright or alludes to it: the power is in the unseen so put your attention there. The 'unseen' that he refers to is the intelligence that is able to create something as spectacular as a Cosmos and everything that it contains. I would like that system to operate me, not my limiting beliefs.

Does it make sense to you, that when the Earth and other planets rotate perfectly around the Sun (without our help, as taught by Sadhguru), that when a seed becomes a mighty tree, that when a child is conceived and then born, doesn't it make sense that some kind of intelligence is behind all of that?

It is wise to recognize the obvious intelligence in the Cosmos. It is intelligent to tap into it. It's an illusion that our own little bit of intelligence is even intelligent. It's a messy mind in love with its unprovable ideas. The mind is not our friend until we master it.

All my perceived powers and my perceived pleasures are all illusions. I see that every time I do any inner work.

We're all busy trying to show everyone how much we know. It's truer that the (unobserved) mind is more ignorant than intelligent. If you doubt that, look at the current state of your mind. Does it control you, or do you control it? Does it give you non-stop peace or prattle?

Everybody talks about, wants, and hopes for oneness, but it's certainly not a constant companion (that we are aware of). We relate to disconnection more than connection or oneness, and yet, there is proof that we are connected to every single thing on the planet and beyond.

"Illusion is the first pleasure." We want the illusion of separateness as our sense of self because we think that's what works and what makes us who we are. "I am an individual." Are we sure that's who we are? It might be in our experience, but does that define us and give us inner joy that can't disappear? It might be a state we aspire to, but is it what causes excessive joy, and once we are separate or independent, do we have permanent joy from it?

We usually only look as far back as our ancestors to determine our connections; or to friends and colleagues, clubs, and gender, to our jobs, our color, our nation and culture, our family, our neighborhood, to anything that our senses land upon and then are processed through false ideas in our heads. We even look to our thoughts, emotions, beliefs, and opinions to determine who we are – but might all of that not be true?

Is who I am the one who gets cranky, bites her cuticles, eats too much, tells white lies, goes to work, and has a house and a car? Is who I am the one who goes on vacations, snaps when she doesn't get her way, has a body I'm not happy with, is a mother, a wife, and a friend? Is who I am the one who has nutty thoughts, feels happy one minute and frustrated the next, is born, and dies – is that who I am? Is that all I am?

As a sidetrack (I made a few) – I get on my knees and thank my body every now and then – for the hard work it does every second of my life. If I have a better body, will I be forever filled with joy? Haha, we humans are so silly. "Illusion is the first pleasure." I have a blind eye. If I can see and it looks like the other one, will that make me forever filled with joy? "Illusion is the first pleasure." I'm so grateful for that blind eye. I can't see out of it and that somehow forced me to begin to see through my heart. There is no illusion in the heart, but the joy for that blind eye is limitless.

Are you on your knees thanking your body? If you do, the Universe will say, "Ah, there's one who gets it, let's bless her/him."

As Sadhguru brings to our attention, we're connected to the moon, the earth, and the sun.

Does it make sense to you that we think of ourselves as individuals and independent, therefore as competitive and disconnected, not cooperative nor deeply connected to everything in existence?

We need to spend a few more minutes on what connection is because, as we've already learned, that's another secret.

It doesn't appear that we are connected to everyone and everything.

WE ARE connected because we breathe the same air.

WE ARE human.

WE LIVE on the same planet.

I am not connected to the rude neighbor, am I? We both want the exact same things in our lives: peace, love, belonging, connection. There are lots of ways we are connected. We both act rudely, and know it feels awful. We're both made of the same stuff, we both have the same bodily functions and needs, and we both know we are going to die one day. We both have the capacity for consciousness that can bring extreme joy or painful ignorance.

WE ARE connected to the trees because they give us the oxygen we need to breathe.

We ARE connected to the stars because we are made of some of the same stuff as they are (look it up, it's science). Stardust falls upon the earth, becomes topsoil, helps grow the food we eat, which then becomes part of us. We exist in the same Cosmos as the stars. When our eyes fall upon them at night, we feel awe, a sense of vastness and deep connection.

WE ARE connected to the moon because it drives the tides on earth and rhythms in a female body. In turn, every person on the planet is connected to a female body because we all were born into physical existence out of one.

WE ARE connected to the Earth, as everything we eat that makes our body comes out of the Earth.

WE ARE connected to the Sun, as it gives us daily life.

If you sit in contemplation for long enough, you will find that there isn't anything that we are not connected to.

"I am an independent life," is an illusion we try to take *pleasure* in. That leads to selfishness as supplying pleasure. Since selfishness can only cause pain, ultimately, it can't be causing true pleasure. The truth is that we are connected to everything and when that is experienced *as* true, we take care of everything. We walk softly on the earth (Sadhguru), hold our hand out to anyone in need, and as a result, fall, heart first, into the lap of peace.

Consciousness is the highest common denominator between all things in the Cosmos. It could be described as the energy that creates. It doesn't make mistakes and it is in everything, That's the biggest connector.

Joseph Campbell suggests that energy and consciousness are the same thing (the unseen). It is impossible to understand that unless you come from a different level of awareness because it's not able to be seen from the intellect. It's not important, except to understand that something created everything – one word for that is consciousness. The grass, humans, the sun, the rivers, rocks; everything was created by something and it had to have awareness of what it was creating for it to turn out as it has. We call that awareness Consciousness.

What created us is often referred to with many names: God, Source, etc. Many of the awakened Masters' use the word Beingness or Isness because we don't have the tendency to 'own' them. We do have the tendency to own our own kind of God, so when that word and what it means doesn't find agreement with another, we fight.

I'm not supposed to talk about God because I might offend you. It's not my intention to offend, it's my intention to share with you that it's critical that you use critical thinking. You are an intelligent human being if you are reading this book and this is something you will want to ponder:

Imagine hollering at someone who has a different God than you do, "This is my God, and he says (you fill in the _____)." The one you're hollering at hollers back at you, "Well this is my God, and he says...)." If there are so many different Gods, which one is real? Can it be true that mine is the real one? What if I was born in another country and that country had a different idea about God? Then that one would be real to me. God is too big a concept for me to understand and I don't need to. I need to keep searching for the truth because that fills me with so much joy I feel like I'm flying free a lot of the time.

We don't make Beingness exclusive to ourselves; each of us IS a Being. We can't argue that. Use whatever word for Beingness that resonates with you, but notice that you don't 'own' it. It exists without our opinion.

Source has the same nature we do: expansiveness, synchronicity, perfection, compassion, and genuineness.

Our True Nature is here waiting for us to tap into it and is not flawed in the same way the Cosmos is not flawed.

Who we are is connected; not independent and not separate.

We unknowingly begin to believe and identify with what we've learned. For example, we identify with being either right or wrong, not with our connectedness. Remember how much trouble we got into when we were wrong as little kids? From that we learned that's who we were: 'I am wrong'. Then we set out to be right, because wrong felt so bad, and that becomes who we think we are. It's a formula for a tug of war - with the point being to be right and find the other wrong instead of relating to their True Nature, and connecting to that.

Notice how we try to fulfill or fix ourselves, and what we put our attention on in an attempt to do that (the illusion is that any of these can fulfill us long-term):

- find a friend
- get married
- become a parent
- get a job
- take a vacation
- make more money
- get a new car, house, phone, etc.
- prove we're right
- judge ourselves and others
- punish ourselves and others
- seek acceptance
- you fill in the _____.

Notice how these things can never take the pain away when we live our lives counting on them to make everything okay.

"Illusion the first pleasure." The illusion is that we are flawed and think we will be fulfilled or fixed by something outside of ourselves.

I hope you are beginning to see that what's flawed is our thinking, not our Being.

Notice how we try to take away the pain we experience:

- avoid the painful feelings
- blame others for how we feel
- abuse alcohol, food, drugs, shopping, etc. to feel better

"Illusion is the first pleasure." Notice how none of those things can take the pain away; they all actually increase the pain. As Guy Finley teaches, they are incapable of delivering what they promise to deliver.

We have a body but were not meant to identify with it, or believe that's who we are. A body comes from two cells that meet, receive nourishment, duplicate, and eventually grow into adult bodies. Sadhguru, logically explains that the body is an accumulation of what comes from the earth. He invites us to consider this: how could we be what we have accumulated? Who we are is not the body. *We do have one* and it is the vehicle for the experiences we are having. Because it's an illusion that WE ARE the body, the body can't give us what we're looking for: unshakable inner peace.

He teaches the same for the mind. It's an accumulation of memories. How can we be what we have accumulated? We're not the mind. We have one. And if you've been paying attention you've begun to notice it goes on and on, making sense a small part of the time, making up painful stories a lot of the time, and isn't good at being quiet or rational. It's an illusion to believe we can get the pleasure we seek from the mind.

Of course, we have a body with its functions, and a mind with its thoughts and emotions, but is there something else that we've missed? Is there something that is unseen that is the bigger part of us?

It's clear that we experience thoughts and emotions, but is that who we are? Thoughts and emotions come from the mind. Since the mind is an accumulation of the past, and, thoughts and emotions come out of the mind, they are repeating the past.

Negative emotions are extensions of thoughts that have more energy in them. That can't be WHO we are even thought we say things like

'I am angry,' 'I am scared,' 'I am worried,' 'I am sad,' 'I am good,' 'I am right(eous),' and 'I am wrong (bad).' When we feel those emotions, we are actually feeling how an identity feels, not how our nature feels.

If those painful thoughts and emotions are who we are, then suffering is the point of life.

That just can't be true.

Life is aliveness. There is never suffering where aliveness truly is.

If life is not about suffering, then what is it and who are we?

That discovery is the purpose of our lives. The challenges life brings each of us, along with the techniques in this book will help uncover it.

Most importantly, with the help of the methods in this book, we will stop unconsciously teaching our children certain ways of living that don't work because we *will stop* living them ourselves.

This book is about teaching ourselves and our kids about ways to uncover who we are and live and love from that place.

Consider this, who we really are is:

— Life in human form.
— A part of Divine Intelligence (since it had a part in creating us).
— Connected to everything that Divine Intelligence created.
— Naturally joyful, compassionate, spontaneous, genuine, harmless, generous, playful; we feel natural in those states, so that is our nature.
— A unique possibility in the evolution of Creation (no two of us the same - quite a feat with billions of people having lived here).

When we have an experience of this, we no longer cling to illusion as the first pleasure. We no longer identify with opinions and beliefs, instead, we want to 'know' and will not rest until we find the truth.

We can't see the truth until we let go of illusions. Much of this work is about exposing illusions so truth can be seen.

There can be no real and lasting pleasure in an illusion.

Two Ways to Exist

Peace or pain, pick one.

When we have ideas, opinions, prejudices, thoughts, or beliefs; we are identified with them. We gain a sense of self from them and work for them, defend them and act them out. If they don't work out or if someone challenges them, we are upset.

That's one way to be in the world.

The other is to connect to Creation and let that be our operating system. Until we are able to do that, it's helpful to know what identities are and how they work.

Identity: An identity is an "Accumulation of memories that excrete out into the future." Sadhguru

— An identity is a long list of perceptions or ideas we have about ourselves. I am good, I am bad, I am right, I am wrong, I am smart, I am dumb, I am rich, I am poor, I am a victim, I am a fixer, I am a healer, I am an accountant, I am a clerk, I am fit, I am serious – as opposed to the peace of having no identity. While these 'I am's' may be in our experience, it's not who we really are.

— An example of an identity is the victim identity. If we have a memory of being a victim, over time, and with repeated experiences where we perceive someone as the perpetrator and ourselves as the victim, we identify with being a victim and view life through that lens. Identifying means that's who we think we are, even though it's not something we think about often or consciously. To keep itself alive, the energy of the victim in us will attract situations that uphold and prove that identity. In other words, our identity as a victim will be why we meet people who attack us and thereby make us the victim. The memory of being a victim sticks until we bring awareness to what we are believing. None of us want to be a victim and yet each of us can tell of a time when we felt that way. Even so, it's not who we are. If we believe it is, victimhood is how we will experience life. I'm not saying horrible things don't happen to us, they do. I'm saying that those one or two minutes that the trauma takes don't need to define us, or determine the pathway our lives will take.

— An identity is an idea that governs us without us knowing it. For example, if we identify with female/male then beliefs attached to that operate us instead of our True Essence. That doesn't mean we aren't having the experience of a female or of a male; it just means that viewpoint doesn't need to govern our experience of life.

— If we have an identity and are attached to being 'good', then we drive ourselves further into division by viewing everything from the good/bad lens. There can't be good without us labelling things as bad, also. There is another lens to see the world through that has no good or bad in it. Seeing anything in life from an identity rather than from the truth IS WHAT CAUSES OUR STRESS. That doesn't mean that things that happen that harm us are okay. People only hurt themselves and others when they are identified. When we view experiences from a step above the level of the mind that sees them as good or bad, we stay centered and can take right action. It's important to note that no one can affect our True Nature. It's untouchable by anything 'bad' we feel has happened to us.

How we (I) know that to be true is when True Nature appears, badness never appears with it.

— An identity is where we falsely gain our sense of self from, and attach ourselves to. It's an idea we have of ourselves to be accepted, successful, safe, and happy. In that process, we ignore the deeper sense of Self, Isness or Being state (the ease of the sense of 'As Is'), the sense of limitlessness, the sense of connectedness, the sense of inclusion, peace and creativity.

— If we are identified with and believing "I am innocent," then we will need others to be perceived as guilty so we can maintain our innocence. That nonsense will take a lot of time and energy. It's much easier to look at an identity or reconnect, than repeatedly live them.

— Most of our attention is given to identities and little of it is given to our natural state of Being.

— Identities are stress-inducing, false ideas, opinions, thoughts, beliefs, and prejudices about who we think we should be to be happy, successful, and safe.

— All identities are provable as false with inner work. All identities are illusions when put up against the truth.

— Identities are hidden in the unconscious mind but show up in our daily lives.

— If we believe we are smart, then we will have a lot of experiences with what we consider dumb people because our smartness needs their dumbness for us to consider ourselves smarter. Worse than that, the identity exerts itself all over everyone else, making them feel dumb so it can look smart.

— Identities are misery-making machines because they can never deliver what they promise in the long-term: fulfillment and peace. This concept is easy to see with addictions. We all have them. Look at something in your life you can't stop but want to (including addicted to thinking). We all believe that whatever it is that we are addicted to, if we get it/use it, we'll fulfill ourselves and feel better. It always turns into pain. The high turns into a low.

— Identities usurp peace and they have to. Peace can't be found in them. That can only be found in truth.

— Living attached to being 'good' or 'right' sets up pain because we count on 'being good' or 'being right' to feel okay. However, in order to have 'good' or 'right', we need to have 'bad' and 'wrong' so that we can gauge/measure them. See the trouble with this thinking that pervades our lives?

— A list of 'should's' and 'shouldn't's' come out of identification. If we believe life should be easy, then we will also believe ideas like: I shouldn't have to work, my body shouldn't have pain, they should do it for me, they shouldn't be mean to me, and so on. These ideas manifest and cause pain. In fact, what we believe (consciously and unconsciously) IS what we manifest.

— All upsetting thoughts and emotions come from identities, not from our True Self.

— We are always in one of two states: identified with truth (True Nature, Beingness, Isness, Divinity, Grace, Divine Intelligence, Source), or identified with beliefs/our lower dual self. There is a paradox here: when we are identified with our True Nature, we feel as though we cease to exist, in a very good way, and are therefore not identified at all. We are Present and alive, but there are no problems visible to us. The world view isn't from the selfish self, but from a place that looks upon 'all that is' with love and compassion.

Ego & Identification

Ego = upset.

All identities/beliefs are ego-based.

Another name for ego is 'personhood' or 'personality', as explained by Mooji. There are two states: personhood or Isness. Isness is the state where there is no identification, no labelling, no judging – with no need for that. It's the recognition of the 'As Is' with regard to everything and everyone.

All negative states are ego-based. All 'false positive' states are ego-based. All natural states are not.

An example of an ego-based state is: if we worry, we are unconsciously believing something like, "I am a good person and show I care if I worry."

An example of a 'false positive' ego-based state is pretending to be happy. That's ego.

Don't be too hard on the ego, that would be the ego being hard on the ego.

Conceiving A Child

The consequences of my own actions...

If you don't have children yet, Osho explains a simple practice to "create the possibility for a higher and more evolved soul to enter into the womb."

"Make love only when you are ready to be in a meditative space. And create a meditative atmosphere while you are making love. You should treat the place as sacred. Creating life... what can be more sacred? Do it as beautifully, as aesthetically, as joyously as possible. There should be no hurry. And if the two lovers meet in such an atmosphere outside, and such a silent space within, they will attract a soul, the highest available."

If it's too late for that, don't worry, the truths in this book can catch you up in a hurry! Besides we all have the same essence in us, so it doesn't matter who ends up as your child. Our job is to uncover and live from our True Nature no matter what kind of child comes into our lives, and no matter what experiences we've had in our own lives.

Source:
http://www.ezinekaleidoscope.com/osho-on-parenting.html

30 Second Parenting Strategy
I Am Important

The more important I am, the more dissatisfaction I have.

Believing we are important causes frustration, anger, and rage (as taught by Guy Finley).

The simple mechanics behind this are:

We learned, as children, that we were unimportant to others and began to identify with being unimportant. That drove us towards trying to be important.

We set out to be important as a way to avoid unimportance.

When I AM IMPORTANT is the hidden operating system, it takes arrogant actions to make itself seem important. When our importance is challenged, we feel anger, frustration, and rage. The anger rises up, we incinerate others and often turn the blast on ourselves.

The degree to which one feels frustration/anger/rage is in proportion to the degree to which one feels important.

The more importance, the more useless the actions are that result from frustration/anger/rage.

One day I was trying to peel off the tape concealing the pin number for my credit card. I didn't read the directions and accidentally destroyed the number. I then proceeded to holler a very nasty word AT THE CREDIT CARD.

Fortunately, I came to my senses and did my work on the issue BEFORE I called the people at the bank, who very patiently explained that the problem was easily solved.

Notice when you feel angry, frustrated or even rage, and notice how important you are at the same time. Notice what a useless thing you are doing (for example: I didn't read the instructions! I'm important and shouldn't have to fool around with a pin number that's difficult to retrieve).

We are relieved from ourselves when we see that we don't need to identify with importance in order to be happy, and that the more important we believe we are, the angrier we will become.

30 Second Parenting Strategy
Parent's Insecurity

Creation created you. No need for insecurity.

Parents often criticize a child's looks, likes, or actions without thinking of the ramifications. It's a bit like bullying. Actually, it is bullying.

Imagine you have a 16-year-old child. Pretend he is going to walk out the door one day to be with friends. You notice he hasn't washed his hair in a while and say to him, "Wash that hair before you leave this house." You're thinking, or maybe saying, "My house, my rules."

You do so because you want him to fit in, be loved. Will it work? If he has clean hair, will he fit in? If the child died tomorrow, would you care about his hair today?

Our focus is on the problem, not the solution. Love finds solutions; criticism doesn't.

It would be more honest to say to the child, after having made such a statement, "Honey, I'm so sorry. I said that because I'm insecure. I think people will think I'm a bad parent. I'm so sorry that I made a fuss over your hair. I love you anyway you look. Your hair is your business." Ten to one the child washes his/her hair soon. Or they won't, but you can stay in a state of love, which is exactly where you want to be.

Has the old way of controlling and manipulating a child ever worked?

It is true that there are still ways to fit into society, and, cleanliness, when it's possible, is one of them. If a child doesn't agree with that, ask them to ask someone who sits beside them if cleanliness matters (Sadhguru's sense of humor!). Our rights do end when they infringe upon another's. Our kids will have to accept the consequences of any actions they take, and that often teaches them a different way.

Bring yourself back to a connected, grounded state before you talk to a child about anything. You will be so glad you did.

30 Second Parenting Strategy
Identity Crisis

"The only crisis we ever have is one of identity."
Guy Finley

It means all upsets are mind-made because we are following our heads, not our hearts; we are unknowingly identifying with a false belief, not with the truth.

Imagine you are a child. Imagine your parents criticize you in an attempt to make you fit in, be acceptable, be successful, and/or be happy, because that's how they were taught by their parents.

You adopt the idea that you are bad, that criticism will make you good, and then you adapt to that belief and live from that place. These ideas group together and become 'identities' that are kept alive even though they are not seen or recognized for the painful strategies they are.

This is one of my favorite exercises for grown-ups and older kids and has been taught to me in many ways by my spiritual teachers. I find immense relief in it, but more importantly, over time, the upsets dissipate when they are put through this technique. It takes practice so don't give up.

1. When you have an upset, use a few words to describe what you are primarily upset about.
2. Close your eyes and take a deep breath.
3. Ask yourself, "What part of me (identity) wants this _____ (fill in with the words you've used to describe the upset)." Wait

for an image or words to appear but don't 'think' them from your intellect.

4. As taught by Guy Finley, consciously suffer the identity and the upset. That means, feel it in your body and your emotions and your mind. You may feel tightening or pain in the body, emotions rise up, and get images of your past. When that passes, move to the next step ONLY IF YOU FELT RELIEF. If you didn't, I suggest you find a Kid Code teacher and get help with this strategy.

The next step is advanced inner work.

1. If the identity is good in your mind (i.e.: I AM HELPFUL), then ask this, "What bad thing does it want for me?" Wait for an image or words to appear but don't 'think' them from your intellect.
2. If the Identity is bad in your mind (I AM STUPID), then ask this, "What good thing does it want for me?" Wait for an image or words to appear but don't 'think' them from your intellect.
3. Work out the formula you've been living by that doesn't serve you or others. Do this by seeing that the identity is causing the upset, so it can achieve something, but that it can't really achieve it.

Example:

Upset: He made fun of me.
What identity needs others to make fun of me?
I AM WORTHLESS.
What good thing does that identity want?
To prove myself.
Recipe for life: In order to prove myself, I must believe that I am worthless, and I do that by needing others to make fun of me. When they make fun of me, that's my internal cue to over-react and try to prove I have worth.

30 Second Parenting Strategy
Setting Intentions (To Gain Clarity)

Clarity is a powerful cure.

This strategy is for setting an intention to bring clarity about your kids and your relationship with them.

Some useful intentions to set that will change the way you relate to children are:

Today it is my intention to see why I'm so critical of my child.
Today it is my intention to see why I worry about my child.
Today it is my intention to see why I want to control my child.
Today it is my intension to see why I punish my child.
Today it is my intension to see why I preach to my child.

Awareness will seep in throughout the day and set you free of ideas that don't work.

30 Second Parenting Strategy
The Event Has No Power

What hurts - is in me.
So, I - can set me free.

Guy Finley teaches that an upsetting event itself has no power. It *is* what it *is*. **The event happens in time and we project the contents of our unconscious mind onto it.**

Said another way, when an event happens that appears to be the cause of our upset, the reality is that the event has nothing to do with how we feel. We are seeing the event through the wounds we haven't healed from our childhood. We are feeling upset because we have a faulty belief that is operating us at that moment, and we are identified with it. What is causing the upset are ideas inside of us not the event.

Eckhart Tolle talks about "Separating the actual event from the interpretation of the event. A thought about an event as dreadful, is merely an illusion of the mind. The situation is neutral, and the unhappiness is optional." I find that hard to understand at times, but also have some experiences of it being true.

An understanding of this is extremely powerful because it puts us in control of our emotional state. If we meet the upset with a strategy designed to reveal the truth – relief is the result. If we don't, more stress (now and later) is the result.

A projection happens when we displace the content of our mind onto someone or something else. We do this because we want to 'get rid' of anything we feel makes us bad or unacceptable.

There are many ways to withdraw the projection and reduce stress. First, we have to remind ourselves that the way we are feeling is because of what's inside of us. That can be a challenge because in almost all situations that upset us, our 'go to' is blame. Blame doesn't heal, it causes more stress.

All self-inquiry methods (quietly looking inside of oneself) withdraws projections.

30 Second Parenting Strategy
The Blessing Boomerang

When you use this, the world will be
full of blessings, because you are.

This strategy is based on two principles 'The world is like it is because I am like I am.' That means whatever we 'put out into the world' is what we will get back.

The other principle is: all beliefs can be 'cleansed'.

When an upset happens, remind yourself that it's coming from the inside (the cause is from a belief on the inside), and the cure is there too.

I have had a lot of scary close calls in vehicles and could never get to the bottom of why people died in vehicles in front of me, why vehicles rolled over in front of me, why people would pass me on the road straight into oncoming semi-trucks.

One day it clicked. I was always cursing at other drivers who make stupid mistakes. That's what I was putting out into the world so what came back to me was to be 'cursed' by other drivers. They had to do stupid things around me because I was literally cursing them every time one of them made a mistake.

The instant I realized that I was getting back what I was putting out, the feeling of cursing another human being overtook me, painfully processed itself through me, and then I, without thinking, began to recite Ho'oponopono. I am sorry (to whatever created me for taking this life that was given freely to me and using it to curse others), please forgive me, thank you, I love you. Nowadays, so far, that's what comes back to me: drivers make way for me and give me a friendly wave: it's quite remarkable to experience such a change (although sometimes I forget myself and lapse into my old pattern for a few seconds!). Seeing I was identified with cursing at others and saying I'm sorry for being identified with that (rather than being identified with Gratitude or Grace), replaced cursing at others on the road.

Ho'oponopono is a cleansing of what doesn't belong in the human being. Dr. Len cured over twenty patients (by looking at their files and repeating the words) of mental disorders in a mental institution.

You don't have to say the words in brackets – I've added those because that's how I experience this work. It's fine to say the original words:

I'm sorry.
Please forgive me.
Thank you.
I love you.

To withdraw projections and change your experience using the Blessing Boomerang and Ho'oponopono:

1. Make a concise statement about a situation that keeps going wrong in your life.
   a. They are rude to me.

2. Be clear on what you are 'getting back' from the Universe.
   a. Example: Rudeness.

3. See how it's true that you are 'putting that out there'.
   a. I'm identified with rudeness:
      i. I act rudely sometimes,

ii. I am upset about it. If I wasn't identified with rudeness, it wouldn't bother me when another was rude.

4. Say the Ho'oponopono words silently:
    a. I'm sorry (I'm identified with rudeness).
    b. Please forgive me (I didn't know that I was identified with rudeness).
    c. Thank you (rudeness, for showing me that is what is causing my pain and causing rudeness to continue to show up in my life).
    d. I love you (Universe, for showing me I'm wrongly identified).

5. Feel all feelings that arise while saying it until they naturally pass.
6. Repeat this process with each new event that arises until you see an amazing change in the events, and you are feeling blessed rather than feeling the need to curse the other or a situation.

Change your experiences in life by changing your internal life. Withdraw your projections one by one and notice that what replaces them is joy.

30 Second Parenting Strategy
Meet Upsets With 'Beingness'

Might there be wisdom inside of me?

John de Ruiter teaches that if you can bring your Beingness to the upset, to the mind, to the thoughts, to the emotions, your heart-based self grows.

To do this:

1. When an upset arises, identify the feeling (worried, betrayed, unloved, angry, etc.).
2. Get in touch with your soft inner Self by putting your attention inside of yourself, and ask if you can bring that (your Beingness) to the feeling, thought or situation. If that's hard for you to do, direct your attention to your heart and wait, asking what it feels like in your heart – paying no attention to the upset at the moment. When you feel a shift into the heart and feel quiet and relaxed, ask yourself if you can bring that state to the upset.
3. Wait and feel the shift to peace.

Emotional Freedom Technique

5 x 5 Rule
If it's not going to mater in five years,
don't spend more than five minutes being upset by it.
-Unknown

That's perfect advice and we need ways to help us achieve that goal. I think five minutes is too long to be upset and give myself a 'wellbeing intervention' by using one of the strategies in *The Kid Code* - to get relief sooner!

EFT is a well-known and extremely effective way to dissolve upsetting emotions quickly. This technique includes tapping on certain points on the body while repeating a specific phrase that includes the upsetting issue.

This system has been so valuable to the Veterans with 85% of them reducing or resolving PTSD and physical pain issues diminishing in 68% of them. Source: https://www.tappingsolutionfoundation.org/tapping-for-war-veterans/

If you search for them on the Internet, you will find that they have a free downloadable manual to explain how to do it. https://eftinternational.org/wp-content/uploads/EFT-International-Free-Tapping-Manual.pdf

There are also videos available on YouTube that will teach you the process in a few minutes.

Reasons to never let an upset (emotional upheaval or a negative state) take you over:

— They drain us of our energy.
— They put strain on or ruin our relationships.
— They cause damage to the physical body (for example, anger causes chemicals that are poisonous to us).
— They are biologically addictive, as previously mentioned.

Happy tapping!

30 Second Parenting Strategy
Pretending

"Lose all wish to pretend."
Guy Finley

"Unless you are playing."
Me

Often times we pretend, so we can be seen in a certain way (that flatters us, makes us look innocent, or makes us look smart, valuable, etc.). We want to uphold an image of ourselves, but, in reality, our True Nature doesn't need us to uphold an image: it's natural, harmless, spontaneous, and compassionate – with all that coming naturally to us, who needs pretense?

Do you like anyone who pretends? Think about someone pretending to be nice through 'constructive criticism' while they are actually just taking an opportunity to criticize you. Think about someone who pretends to help you while they are really doing whatever they're doing so they can bolster their own ego.

No one likes pretense.

Pretending to be something else undermines stability.

When there is no pretense, there is a solid place to be. If we pretend, it will take us a long time to find ease within.

Notice that pretense is transparent. It's easy for us to see through another's pretense. It's as easy for others to see through ours.

Notice the uselessness of pretense and stop right as you notice. Take a breath and start the conversation or action over.

30 Second Parenting Strategy
Getting Honest

Being honest may not get you a lot of friends,
But it will always get you the right ones.
                                            -John Lennon

We want our kids to be honest with us.

They want us to be honest with them.

The reason for that is because honesty is in our nature and dishonesty isn't. There is so much strength, integrity, and healing vulnerability in honesty.

When we are dishonest, we are training our kids to lie.

When we are dishonest, we are undermining ourselves, hiding ourselves, and unwilling to really stand for what works for us.

When you don't know something, be honest and say you don't know. Don't make something up. Notice that it's way less stressful to say 'I don't know' without judging ourselves, than it is to make something up.

Tell your kids you are working out how to parent them best; admit that you don't know everything.

Tell them when you make a mistake.

Honesty never causes stress. If there is negativity in a relationship or conversation, honesty hasn't been reached. Keep working at what you

really need to say or do until the negativity has disappeared. That's the time to talk to another.

I say to people who drive really fast, "I have a problem in vehicles. I don't feel safe because I have been in so many car accidents when another person was driving, and I over-react which will cause us both stress. Would you mind helping me by driving more slowly?" Most people have agreed to help me. I'm not criticizing their driving, but I'm sharing my own problems in a vehicle. It's better than not saying anything, and because it's my problem and not theirs, it's usually received well.

I gave that example because if you have a 'real' conversation make sure to tell the truth and not blame. If it's a blame, it's not the truth.

The way to end dishonesty is to stop yourself when you feel it happening see that it's not really helping and start over.

30 Second Parenting Strategy
People Pleasing

People pleasing makes us unpleasant.

All of us do it and wish we didn't.

Notice that all the approval we've gotten from others hasn't made us whole or happy. Notice that people-pleasing turns us into the opposite: we begin to dislike the people we are trying to please.

Sit quietly for a moment and ask yourself this question every day for a month:

Where am I fake, and trying to please others so they'll like me or, so I'll get something I want?

You will get:

— images
— sensations in your body
— emotions
— slideshows in the mind of where you have been fake

Sit with whatever comes up and feel the feelings until they pass, as they always do; seeing ends being. When we 'see' ourselves, if it's not natural to us, it has to dissolve. Being fake and trying to please others is not natural. That doesn't mean we don't help or care about others: true service to others is natural to us and there isn't an ounce of fakeness in it.

This is a wonderful exercise to bring yourself into awareness around the roles you unconsciously adopt around certain people, so you can convince both of you that you are pleasing.

It takes a lot of energy to uphold something that isn't natural.

30 Second Parenting Strategy
Listening

*"We have two ears and one mouth for a reason:
to listen twice as much as we speak."*

Anonymous

Interrupting anyone means that you believe you are more important than them, as taught by Guy Finley. Learn to stop and apologize when you interrupt your child and ask them to continue.

Are you more important than your child (or anyone else)?

If you really listen and look in their eyes, you will create connection.

Suzi Lula teaches a method of 'sacred listening'. It means to come into your highest self, give your full attention to others, don't interrupt, and give others space to talk.

30 Second Parenting Strategy
Keeping Your Kids Quotes

Kids brighten our lives with their words.

Your child will say things that you wish they didn't, and other times what they say will light up your life in ways that nothing else can.

Catching the lighter side of life and keeping your 'kid-quotes' in a journal only takes a few minutes and will give everyone in your family joy for years to come. You can pull it out when you've had a hard day, when they've had a hard day, read it together monthly, or you can make it into a gift for graduation day.

Buy an inexpensive, lined scribbler and keep it so it's handy to record the moments that make memories. With each entry, put the date, who said it, and what they said.

I kept my book by my bed and when the kids were older, I let them read it – just before they graduated from high school. They didn't know I had written down those wonderful things about them. They laughed, and they cried, and they knew, without a doubt, how much they were loved, in spite of my poor parenting skills.

There are some things we just don't want to forget, and keeping track of their innocent and heart-warming words will bring them and you a lot of joy.

These are some quotes from my grandkids:

Lily (age 6):   Grandma, did you know Macy ate a worm?

Me: a real worm?

Lily: yup.

Me: Macy did you eat a worm?

Macy: No, I just kissed it.

Lucy (age 4):   What happens when you die, Grama?

Me: I don't know, I'm not there yet.

Lucy: does anybody know?

Me: nobody I know, knows.

Lucy: not even Google?

Jess (age 10 upon arriving in Mexico at the beach): I miss the sound of flip flops.

Ivy (age 8 upon looking in the mailbox and finding a box of chocolates): Mom, I thought after we put the sign in our box, 'No junk mail" we aren't supposed to get junk?

Ruby (upon feeling tension between the adults in the kitchen while cooking a meal): The heart glows, Grama.

Macy (age 4 while poking about at my hair): Grama did you paint your hair white?

30 Second Parenting Strategy
A Child's Ideas

A person is a person, no matter how small.
                                                    -Dr. Seuss

Very young children have great ideas and often come up with them at just the right time. Listen to them and get caught up in the fun of their ideas. Often times their ideas are simple such as, "Let's go outside and play." If there isn't a good reason not to, follow their lead. It's how they become creative leaders. If you follow their lead once, then they will continue to come up with creative, spontaneous ideas.

On one emotionally hard day for my family, one of the grandkids popped up and said we should go make sandcastles. No one felt like it. Feeling morose had us immobile. Fortunately, we couldn't resist that innocent little face and we went out with her and morose morphed into magic.

When you're lost about life, ask a child, "What should we do?" They might have a good idea.

30 Second Parenting Strategy
Trust Your Kids' Intelligence

Intelligence is innate.

We think that when we 'learn' we are becoming intelligent. The underlying intelligence in a human being IS what allows us to learn.

Intelligence blossoms under the right conditions.

One day, when I was driving my granddaughter, Ivy, to daycare, I couldn't remember exactly where it was (it was in a city I wasn't familiar with). Ivy said to me, "Grama, I know how to get there." She was four at the time and I thought I might be considered a bit nutty if I asked her to give me directions. I came to my senses and grinned at her in the rear-view mirror and said, "Show me the way, Ivy Joy," and she did. From the back seat, in a car seat, a four-year-old can give directions that are a bit complicated. Children are amazingly intelligent. All of them.

I didn't realize it at the time, but later, upon reflection, I came to understand that we often 'dumb down' our kids by not letting them use their intelligence. If I'd ignored Ivy, even though she did know how to get to the day care, and called her mom or dad for directions, I would have contributed to teaching her that she should be doubted.

If it doesn't work out (they make a mistake), refer to the 30 Second Parenting Strategy: Blessing Mistakes.

30 Second Parenting Strategy
All the World's A Stage

"All the world's a stage,
And all the men and women merely players;
They have their exits and their entrances,
And one man in his time plays many parts…"
-William Shakespeare

Our childhood experiences teach us many lessons. The lessons keep us safe, keep a roof over our heads, clothes on our back, and teach us how to get love and acceptance from others – we think. We have no idea that acceptance is actually our job alone.

Most of the lessons we learned that play out throughout our adult lives happen without us being aware that we are acting out faulty pre-recorded scripts written long ago. These scripts are stored in our unconscious minds and repeat like a broken record without us noticing. Did you ever wonder why we repeat relationship patterns even when we change who we are in relationship with? The information was absorbed and stored as a child and is now doing the only thing it knows how to: repeat. Not only that, the script can't deliver what it promises: safety, happiness, etc.

Here's an example of a lesson we learn in childhood: I'm bad when I don't do what the adults say, and if I am punished, I will learn to be a better person.

This lesson translates, in our adult years into another role that we assume without knowing it: Good Punisher. We, as Good Punishers, set out in the world to make everyone, including ourselves, good people by punishing them or ourselves.

The Good Punisher role has a problem: punishment teaches punishment. Abuse teaches abuse. It's hard to imagine what would happen if we didn't punish or scold another. How would we get 'good people?'

If we are clear in our minds, have no roles to play, and are authentic, we don't need to be told how to act or what to think; love and its actions come naturally. Our True Nature knows what to do, and the doing turns out to serve everyone and hurt no one.

Some of the unconscious roles that pop up into our day, and that dictate our thinking, our perception, our words, our feelings, and our actions are:

— good girl/good boy
— bad girl/bad boy
— smart girl/smart boy
— stupid girl/stupid boy
— strong girl/strong boy
— weak girl/weak boy
— savior/destroyer
— know-it-all/dummy
— victim/perpetrator
— bully/victim
— important/unimportant
— you fill in the _____

Try this exercise and see what happens:

Notice yourself becoming an actor. Notice the role you are playing. Notice the actions and words necessary to keep the role. Notice how you feel. Notice how others are around you. Noticing is enough to begin change without doing anything else. Your nature knows what to do without ever adopting a role.

You'll know you're acting, or in a role because you won't feel natural. You'll feel like something is off and feel stress.

In that moment, change your life by quitting the acting job, take a breath and start over from a genuine place. Once you do this exercise once, you'll want to do it forever.

When you are genuine, without roles to play, you will be at ease.

30 Second Parenting Strategy
Fighting Over Food

No one wins in a fight.

On a day when you're not hungry, make a meal you don't like and eat the whole thing. Why do we feed kids things they don't like? We don't like eating what we don't like.

Parents primarily fight with their children over food because they want to be a good parent and keeping their children healthy is one way to do that. Read that statement until you understand that it's the same as saying good parenting requires fighting (over food or anything else) with kids.

Fighting has never been best for anybody.

Parents fight with their kids about food out of fear that their kids will get sick.

No matter what you feed your child, your child will ultimately be challenged with some kind of ache or pain, or health issue in their lifetime, and you can't stop challenges. Challenges will grow them into who they really want to be: conscious human beings. Look at the children who have already grown up. They have challenges, no matter what they were fed. If they eat their broccoli, will they then not get sick - ever? Do you know anyone who hasn't gotten sick at some point? A physical body, by its nature, experiences physical troubles.

It's also true that live-giving food IS life giving.

A gripping desire to control what kids eat stems from fear. The Universe gives and takes life. Now that this is clear, the more practical way to approach food is to make them what they like within obvious limits. Let them try all kinds of new foods, and, feed them when they are hungry. Kids don't care if 'it's time to eat'.

Stop making kids eat what they don't like. It's not good for you or them. "One bite - to see if it's right" works because kids sometimes surprise themselves, and us, and like something that we make that's healthy! They may not like broccoli or green things now, but they may love them later.

When I babysit my grandchildren, I don't fight over food. I don't keep junk food in the house (if I did, I'd eat it) so there is never anything to fight over. There is a variety of foods that they can choose from, and they can eat it whenever they choose. They are the best judge of when they are hungry and what they are hungry for. Sometimes they eat three times in the morning, a bit in the afternoon, and then don't eat much supper. Sometimes it's the opposite. If meal time does require some regulation, it's okay to do that too (sometimes we have to regulate meal times).

That doesn't mean I don't ever give them junk food – but it's rare. My associate degree is in holistic nutrition and sometimes I use that education!

If you don't have junk, processed, and sugar-laden foods in your house, but you do have lots of whole and fresh foods, kids will eat it. And, as my daughter, Kerri says, "It's the decisions over the long term that matter." Some treats are okay.

30 Second Parenting Strategy
Gratitude for The Body

The body has been working for us for our whole lives.

One day, I was sitting in the bathtub with my 3-year-old granddaughter, when she climbed up on my lap. She sat there with her thumb in her mouth, leaning against me, both of us cuddling in the warm water, not saying anything, just sitting together. She turned and then took both of my breasts in her tiny little hands, and, in a very serious voice, while pushing my fifty-four-year-old breasts upwards, said, "Grama your muscles are falling."

That brought a different perspective to my body image and aging.

Out of the mouths of babes, and right to the point.

Even though she was hoisting my 'falling muscles' upward she spoke as though there was nothing wrong. She was simply pointing out what she observed. Kind of like saying how the bathwater is warm, the plant is green, the sky is blue, night follows day, your 'muscles' are falling.

She taught me that anything can be said when it's the simple truth. When it's said with the absence of judgment, it will be received as it is given: in innocence. The truth contains no malice. If you say something that feels malicious, you know it's not the truth.

With the absence of judgment in her statement, I had a deep realization: judging the body is disrespectful to that which created us. Bodies aren't made to be judged. They are important, and, at the same time, they are not 'who we are'. They are the container for the Being part of us. They come in all shapes, sizes, and colors.

If there is every shape, size, and color what's the point of judging?

If you Google 'National Geographic' regarding the subject of race, they say there is no such thing. Skin color is simply adaptation, nothing to do with race. Humans began in Africa and we spread out over the world adapting our skin color depending on our geographical location. Should we judge our skin color of the color of another's skin, or could we have gratitude for it?

Judging a body for any reason is useless.

It's a good idea to teach children that there is not anything wrong with their body no matter how a body shows up.

Another lesson my grandkids taught me is this: in the early hours of the morning, I was standing in the kitchen in my nightie when I heard the pitter patter of little feet coming up the stairs.

Two little blonde heads appeared as they peeked around the corner to see who was in the kitchen. When they saw me, they laughed, and ran towards me, one lifting up my nightie in the front and ducking under, and the other lifting up my nightie in the back and ducking under.

I stood frozen for a moment. I had nothing on under my nightie. As it turns out, they didn't care what they saw. One patted my belly, the other patted my bum, and they moved around me, making a tent out of the nightie as they danced around me, happily patting.

I learned something important on that day.

Teach your child that differences such as big noses, small chins, fat bodies, skinny bodies, skin color - don't matter. They certainly don't matter to little kids. They can't see through judgmental eyes.

The perfect body doesn't exist. And, every body is perfect enough as it is; as long as it's breathing, it's pretty good.

Judgment is separation; it is so outdated. It's also beneath us. Loving one another is the only thing that works.

How to teach them healthy body image is to model it for them. Accept your body right now. Say it to yourself, "I accept my body. It can't be any other way at this moment than it is. I accept my body." All else is madness (to use Eckhart's phraseology).

For a moment, right now, look at your body and thank it for all it has done for you. The reversal from judgment to gratitude puts us into 'right thinking'.

30 Second Parenting Strategy
Individual Attention

If you give kids a lot of attention,
they won't need a lot of anything else.

To foster bonding, take time to have individual time with each child separately. Arrange this with willing grandparents and others, also.

Good parenting takes time and the time we spend with our kids pays off with a closer connection. That makes solving problems easier.

30 Second Parenting Strategy
The Unconscious Comes Calling – I Can't Sleep!

Resisting messages = resisting peace.

Parents need their sleep.

Byron Katie says that we don't sleep if we don't have a clear conscience. That means if we wake in the night, we may have something on our mind that needs us to bring awareness to it.

There are obvious exceptions: if you wake up because of a loud sound, for example, it's not likely that you need to do any inner work unless fear comes up.

Make a note of what's on your mind when it keeps you from sleeping or wakes you up.

— Do the work immediately (use one of these strategies), or,
— Make a note of what's on your mind and do it the next day.

Could it be that simple? Try this and see how your sleep improves. I used to wake up many times every night. Because I do my own inner work on any upset that happens in the day, I go to sleep easily and rarely wake up in the night.

30 Second Parenting Strategy
Jealousy

Jealousy dissolves when comparison does.

Kids will suffer from jealousy just like we do.

Jealousy happens because of a mind that compares. Kids often express jealousy and we don't constructively know what to do about it.

Teach them this:

We are unique. If you look around you, do you see another person like you? I am ME. I have WHAT I HAVE. I LOOK HOW I LOOK. How do I know that's true? Because all of what I am makes me, ME. I wouldn't be me if it were up to me, I'd morph myself into what I think will make me happy. That's where the trouble starts because I believe that what the other is or has will make me happy.

One has to ask this simple question: If I get what I want, am I really happy in the long-term? Will that happen with a car, a body shape, shoes, a haircut, or money? If it hasn't so far, then it probably never will. That's reason enough to look in another direction. That's not to say you shouldn't get the new car, keep healthy, etc. However, don't count on those things for long-term joy. It's not their job.

We are jealous because of what we think we want that others have: a good job, nice hair, a kind personality, money, health, a nice house, fun, etc.

Jealousy can only happen when we don't see what we have ourselves.

When you want something others have, look to see if you might not already have it.

Here's an example: "I want those shoes. I'm jealous." What do those shoes mean to me and how do I already have that? The shoes may mean that I am okay, acceptable.

Am I already acceptable, even without the shoes? The answer, if it comes from deep within, will always be yes.

You will see that you already have what you think you want and that stops the wanting. As the Buddha said, "Wanting is our only problem." When we stop wanting, we stop creating a lot of problems.

'Having' won't cause inner joy.

You have your own life. You are a flower waiting to blossom; tend what you have been given.

Comparison takes away from your blossoming self.

Keep your focus on your connecting` not comparison.

30 Second Parenting Strategy
Lying, The Cause & The Cure

*The liar's punishment is not in the
least that he is not believed,
but that he cannot believe anyone else.*
        -George Bernard Shaw

Lying causes a lot of stress.

**When you notice you are telling a lie, pay attention and notice the
stress you feel arising inside of yourself.** Don't judge yourself, just notice.

Lie detectors demonstrate this: the stress response shoots up when
we lie.

Besides reducing stress, another benefit to ending lies is that you
become clear yourself and can tell truth from lies. It's nice to know
when the other, internet information or information in a book is not
truthful; it guides you.

It's not that we have to call the other out when they lie, it's more
important to know and respond accordingly. Or, if it is necessary to
say something, doing it with kindness will feel better for both of you.

There are 'bad' reasons to lie that seem like 'good' reasons to lie.

Lying comes from being identified so it's necessary for a conscious person
to understand that almost everyone is going to lie. It is not necessary to
get entangled in it or upset by it. Accept that the other is lying in a false
attempt to help themselves, and that they might not even notice they are

lying. They don't know telling the lie won't really help them, and will cause even more stress when they have to keep acting as though the lie is true. An example would be to tell someone you like something they like in a bid for acceptance or to look good, but you don't really like it. You might tell someone you like camping, scary movies, documentaries, or that you'd love to do something that you don't want to do, etc. when you really don't. The moment the lie is out of our mouths, it becomes stressful because it's out of alignment with Creation, has to be upheld, and is almost always exposed (which cause us more stress).

If you keep the lie hidden you feel pressure inside of yourself. You also feel stress and you end up doing things that cause you more stress, like having to watch a scary movie because you said you liked them when you don't.

Reasons we lie:

— To try and keep ourselves out of trouble. Lying doesn't keep us out of trouble, though, it SEEDS trouble into us (as taught by Guy Finley). A lie strengthens the ego/identities which is the source of pain within us.

— To try to get approval from others. Look at all the approval we've gotten over time from different people that didn't make us happy in the long run. If I am dependent on others for my happiness and I lie to get their approval, then I am dependent upon lying to make myself happy. Lying does not gain us approval NOR does it make us happy. Both of those states, happiness and clarity that brings true confidence, come from a balanced inner life.

— We lie because we don't trust others. Lying won't solve the trust problem. We trust in the wrong things: having a nice house, making lots of money, etc. We trust the other will make us happy. Find true things to trust in, such as: The Universe knows better than I do, people are identified and will speak and act from that place, natural feels good, nature heals us, we are only a part of life here, death of the physical body is certain but since the Universe is sending everything to us, for us, then that's got to be good too. Trust in those things.

— We lie because we don't know that the truth is always about ourselves, not others. As I mentioned earlier, I tell people I ride with that I'm a nervous rider and apologize for my nervous reactions. I also tell them that my reactions bother me and I'm working on that issue. I have been involved in a few motor vehicle accidents where people died. While I'm in a car, my subconscious mind still believes I'm in danger on some level. If I tell the other they are not driving appropriately, I'm not being honest. They must be driving okay since I'm not injured or dead yet. A clear mind is a wonderful gift. It ends blame and lets us look at what the real issues are and only then can we make headway. If I lie and say they are driving recklessly when the truth is that I'm believing unconscious thoughts, I will have more stress (and possibly get kicked out of the car!).

— We lie because we think we are smarter than others and think we can get away with it.

We teach kids to lie for the above reasons but for these reasons as well:

— To get love they say what they think we want to hear. We set them up by unconsciously teaching them that they are unlovable and bad – in other words, we teach them that they ARE their behaviors and then they operate from that perspective. The cure is to teach them that they are a Being with behaviors that are going to appear for the purpose of waking them up into consciousness. Their Being takes care of the 'getting love' issue.

— To keep from being punished. Do you remember lying to keep from being punished? If we didn't punish with such rigid condemnation, and absolute conviction that we are right to punish them, they wouldn't be so afraid of it and feel they have to lie.

— They are afraid they won't be safe, that they might be abandoned: mentally, emotionally, or physically. Children don't feel secure in this world once they start to believe the conditioning, we teach them, unless they are reminded how to experience deep connection.

— It appears easier. It appears to avoid conflict but creates more conflict.

Say to your kids, "I see that you feel you need to tell me a lie. Can you tell me why?" Let them answer the best they can. Don't put words in their mouths to 'make everything okay' because that will send the troubles underground to surface another time. Help them by reassuring them that *they aren't* in trouble, that they may have consequences as all actions do, but that they are loved. Also tell them that and you don't want them to have the stress that lying causes them.

Trouble is inevitable if we lie. Lying may appear to get us out of trouble in the moment, but it gets us into trouble with ourselves because we aren't being honest. That means we are saying it's not okay to be ourselves and then we set out to NOT BE OURSELVES. That's not good for us.

No one approves of someone who lies. Think of someone who lies to you. It brings up all sorts of feelings ranging from discomfort and dismissal of them to outright anger.

What we are attempting to achieve by lying is not really being achieved.

When a child lies, don't lecture them about lying. Rather, tell them that lying is self-betrayal. Lying means they are not supporting themselves.

They can't BE themselves if they lie in an attempt to get approval or avoid trouble.

BEING THEMSELVES is more important than lying.

Everyone loves honesty because it's natural.

30 Second Parenting Strategy
Act as Though You Chose Whatever Happens

*"Having children is like living in a frat
house - nobody sleeps, everything's broken,
and there's a lot of throwing up."*
                                    -Ray Romano

What we need to trust in is that life is happening for us, not to us (Byron Katie). That means that the Universe is delivering to us exactly what we need to bring us into peaceful consciousness.

Eckhart Tolle teaches this simple stress-relieving method: if something happens in your life that you don't like, act as though you chose it.

Since the thing we don't like has already happened or is happening, it's insane to argue with it. As Katie says, if you argue with reality, you lose, but only one hundred percent of the time.

Sadhguru teaches us that this moment in front of us right now is inevitable. Recognizing that can help us out of stories and big useless emotions that arise, and then we can look at the moment with curiosity and learn what we need to.

When your kids are acting like frat-brats, pretend you chose it. Oh, wait, we did! But, we can't send them back, so use your favorite strategy to keep your sane while the nonsense goes on.

Since life is happening for me, if I'm upset about something, I remind myself it happened for me. Then I use one of the strategies in this book, and I work the upset. **That it happened *for* me proves out every time.** Every single thing that has happened to me has been to bring me into awareness.

30 Second Parenting Strategy
Making Friends with Your Kids Through Play

Get your 'happy' back.

My dad, at age 96, played hide and seek with his great grandkids. They loved him. He knew a secret: play makes friends.

If you want to have a good relationship with kids, make friends with them by playing with them every chance you get – at least once per day. Make a daily designated time for play time, even if it's short.

Kids will play with anyone who will play with them.

When they are little that means getting down on the floor and playing with them.

When they are big, that means doing things they like. We might find that we like it too because everybody likes playing, once we get over stories, excuses, and limitations. Playing is built into each of us. You will be surprised at the capacity and capabilities we have once we step out of our comfort zone, (which isn't all that comfortable).

30 Second Parenting Strategy
Being Friends with Your Kids

Friendship is just connection.

There is a modern philosophy that you can't be friends to your kids.

We sure don't want to be enemies with them. It's true that we will not be exactly the same as their peers in terms of friendship, *and* we don't need to be.

This fad of stating that we aren't friends with our kids has come about because parents don't know what to do with their kids other than punish them when they act out. What some call tough love, I call giving natural consequences without overreacting myself. All of our decisions won't be easy to make but they can be made with love.

If we don't believe we need to punish them, we CAN BE FRIENDS with our kids.

Even if we slip and do punish our children, we can see the error of our ways, see that punishment isn't getting us what we really want, which is a good relationship with our children as we both go through all of life's trials.

Not punishing a child doesn't excuse children from being responsible for their actions: they, like us, are 100% responsible for their behaviors and actions and the resulting consequences.

We can make amends for punishing anyone at any time. Punishment has never brought about good behavior. True goodness and 'good' behavior come from our True Nature.

Gently correcting a child is necessary, is a natural and comfortable skill, and maintains friendship because the correction leads the child to feeling good about themselves. For me, correction is more accurately described as sharing. "This is what happened to me when I did that." "There is a consequence with that, it's okay if you want the consequence."

When we gently correct a child, we are looking after our own wellbeing too.

30 Second Parenting Strategy
Who Does My Child's Life Belong To?

"There are two lives being lived."
-Rainer Maria Rilke

In a family, there are many lives being lived.

Look at children through these eyes and see what a difference it makes in how you feel about them, how you parent them, and how you show love to them.

See everyone in your family (and all others) as a life being lived; their own life.

30 Second Parenting Strategy
Do What You Love

*"Choose a job you love, and you will
never have to work a day in your life."*
— *Confucius*

While Sadhguru's lesson on this is a bit stronger, it's true: Idiots hate their job, intelligent people love their job, genius's love whatever is in front of them.

It's really insane to stay in a job you don't like. As Eckhart Tolle says, we need to accept it or change it. All else is madness.

Complaining about it and hating it won't change it.

If you love what you do, it loves you back.

If you want your children to blossom and to spend their time doing what they love, lead by example and find a job you love.

If you can't change jobs, change your mind, and make it a fantastic place for you to be. Think of one way you can make your job into something you love and do it today. If you can't think of how to do that, do Byron Katie's 'The Work' on every single thing about your job that you hate. Soon you will be wanting to kiss the feet of those 'awful people' and 'terrible situations' because of what you'll learn about yourself and free yourself from.

30 Second Parenting Strategy
Nature

Nature IS nurture.

Take yourself and your kids out into Nature as much as you can. Kids can explore and play out there for very long periods of time and its good for them.

It's a good place to connect with your own True Nature, too. The reason for this is that what we see in nature touches a corresponding part inside of us (as taught by Guy Finley). It touches that part of our nature that is peaceful and free. That's why it feels so good to be out there.

When we see something outside of us, we feel it inside of us where it pre-exists.

That's also how we know we are more than our bodies, our minds, and our emotions. We can feel it most easily when we're in nature.

Nature is also a balancing and harmonizing agent, as taught by Eckhart Tolle. That means when we are in nature, we can come into balance in our minds, bodies, and emotions. Having experienced this many times, I want to run outside right now!

Think about how you feel watching the water run over the stones in a creek or gazing at a mountain peak and being drawn into the moment where stillness exists. During those times, we are transfixed by an outer appearance that catalyzes and corresponds to an inner state.

This is Presence, the gift of Timelessness, our focus brought to a single moment that captures us. In this place, troubles melt away.

Nature is rapture. Go get some every day. It's free and abundant in the great outdoors.

30 Second Parenting Strategy
"Oops Means Opportunity"

There's never a good reason to be
upset. It's not good for you.

Barney Saltzberg, author of *Beautiful Oops*, offers this idea:

"When a child spills something, or makes what we would call a mistake, use it; don't lose it!"

When my granddaughter, Ruby, spilled milk on the floor, my daughter, Amanda, used that strategy, after learning about *Beautiful Oops*, and used the mess as an opportunity to teach responsibility, stay calm, AND have some fun. It's essential to understand that the child doesn't do those things intentionally. Making them feel bad won't help them or us.

See if the shape of the spill makes an animal or a letter of the alphabet.

Is it not possible to both teach the child to wipe the mess up her/himself, and have a look-see at what creativity might pop up at the same time?

Who hasn't made a mess? Who wishes to be treated with understanding when they do?

Using this strategy is just easier on everyone. Isn't that what we want: way less tension?

And don't forget to use Blessing Mistakes!

30 Second Parenting Strategy
Stubbornness

Stubbornness is a weak proclamation: I'm right.

Stubborn people can be very difficult to work with.

The bad news is that we are all stubborn.

Stubbornness works hand-in-hand with false flexibility/being too agreeable. They are two sides of the same coin. When one side is operating us, we have no flexibility. When the other side is operating us, we have no boundaries.

When someone is stubborn, we want them to be flexible and do what we say! I hope you can see the contradiction in that statement. We stubbornly want the other to be flexible.

The union of stubbornness and flexibility yields a practically persistent approach to life. Practical persistence is doing what serves everyone in the situation. This is a valuable attribute in a person's life because it aids us with our daily achievements.

Notice when stubbornness arises. Notice that you are stubborn about your child's stubbornness. Notice that doesn't resolve the situation. Notice that you are hoping the child will be flexible/agreeable with your stubbornness. See where you are being stubborn and take a breath. A practical solution is likely to present itself with a moment of reflection.

My granddaughter, Ruby, at age two and half showed me this valuable lesson. She was sticking her fingers in the humidifier. When I told her to get her fingers out and move away, she just sat there looking at me. I didn't even look closely to see if she could stick her fingers in and get them hurt, or if there was something protecting little fingers that might wander that way. I was busy doing something when this situation happened, and I asked her to move away without checking it. She moved her fingers out but didn't move away so I slid her little bottom about a foot away and frowned my disapproval at her. She just stared at me. Her stare told me to stop myself.

I knew it was a teacher/student moment with me being the student. I realized that I was stubborn about insisting she move away, and she was stubborn about not moving. She had to reflect my stubbornness back to me. And she did! I wasn't practically persistent, which would have served everyone. A practically persistent person would see if there were danger, not assume, and not stubbornly move the child to safety even if there is no danger, not stubbornly hold to their (my) own unproven opinion. As soon as I understood this, I put my hand down to take hers and she put her little hand in mine, and we went off and played. The stress dissipated immediately. Lesson learned.

As soon as my 'will' is put away, I come back to sanity.

30 Second Parenting Strategy
Accepting Our Children

They are who they are.

Accept your child as the Being they are (as taught by Dr. Shefali). They are just like us: currently experiencing identities and acting them out. Do it now. Say to yourself, "I accept my child as they are." Anything else is madness (to quote Eckhart, again)!

That doesn't mean their bad behavior is serving them or anyone else. It means you accept them and free yourself of the stress of non-acceptance. Behavior can still be addressed. They are not their behavior, and they are responsible for it, just like we are.

30 Second Parenting Strategy
Pushing Our Children to The Extraordinary

Blossom them into whatever they were meant to be.

We all want successful children, but it never occurs to us that they have their own success built into them. One of our jobs as parents is to make sure we don't obscure the light inside of them. Are we sure we know what's best for them? Might our version of their life not be right for them? Be supportive of yourself, and of them, by asking these questions instead of insisting you know.

Dr. Shefali teaches that:

"Scarcity in ourselves is what makes us project our desires onto our children and push them to excellence and greatness. This causes suffering in children. They burn out and take anti-depressants because we are all drinking the Kool-Aid that says our children need to become something, rather than unfold into their own greatness."

Source:
https://www.youtube.com/watch?v=LMVV2XUvWkU

Notice your expectations of your children and reflect back on what it felt like for your parents to 'run' or 'interfere with' your life. A minute of two of contemplation will help you see that you wanted to be your own person and so does your child. Help them to become that.

I know a man who didn't care for school so he quit early and has happily driven a garbage truck for thirty-seven years. He figured out quickly what happiness was and what it wasn't. He blossomed himself.

30 Second Parenting Strategy
Sharing Our Dragons

A problem shared is a problem halved.
Ancient proverb

Problems get bigger when they are hidden and shrink when they're shared.

In the hit movie, "Crocodile Dundee" there is a scene that demonstrates a simple truth: sharing a problem shrinks the problem. When we share a problem, we feel less alone, less disconnected, less burdened, and we get to 'face' the problem instead of staying stuck *in* the problem itself.

Excerpt:
"**Sue Charlton**: People go to a psychiatrist to talk about their problems. She just needed to unload them. You know, bring them out in the open.
Michael J. "Crocodile" Dundee: Hasn't she got any mates?
Sue Charlton: You're right. I guess we could all use more mates. I suppose you don't have any shrinks at Walkabout Creek.
Michael J. "Crocodile" Dundee: Nah ‑ ‑ back there, if you got a problem, you tell Wally. And he tells everyone in town... brings it out in the open... no more problem."

Encourage your children to talk about any problem they have. Let them speak without interrupting them.

Kids don't want to talk about problems to someone who is going to criticize, judge and punish, that's why they go to their friends and not their parents. Don't be that person if you want your kids to talk to you about problems.

There is nothing like having one hundred percent of another's genuine, non-judgmental attention when you need it.

Do you remember someone looking at you with love in their eyes while you spoke? That compassion, directed at you when you have a problem, is connection. Connection, all by itself, *is* a problem solver.

In speaking openly to a non-judgmental person, we are able to bring more clarity to our problems, even if they don't say a word.

Once a problem is shared, the tension lessens and it's easier to focus on a solution.

30 Second Parenting Strategy
Give Kids the Floor

Following them is fun!

In the (very) early hours of the morning before the sun was even close to rising, my granddaughter, Lily, crawled into bed with me. She cuddled for a minute and I felt the bliss. I know that if I'm quiet, whoever has come to visit will either teach me something, make me laugh, or melt my heart, if not all three. Lily was true to form. I stayed quiet, holding her, and then she sat straight up, looked at me and said, "Grama, do you want to do this with me?" and then she stuck her tongue out and kept it there.

What could I say? Of course I wanted to do that with her.

If you be quiet, kids will engage the best parts of you. We don't need to be the one in charge, control the conversation, or show off how much we think we know.

30 Second Parenting Strategy
Am I Being Me?

Be yourself, everyone else is already taken.
-Oscar Wilde

My daughter, Kerri, taught me a wonderful way to deal with children who are acting out.

When her daughters act out, she has them ask themselves 3 questions:

— "Am I being Me?"
— "Am I respecting boundaries?"
— "Am I getting the kind of attention I want?"

This way of turning the child's attention inward ends the upset and points them to right action that serves.

I love to watch this process because they can see that their own actions aren't serving them, especially when they disrespect the boundaries of another person. For example, they might want attention, but are pulling down on your shirt so hard it's putting you off balance. You can't give the attention they need, and they don't get the attention they need.

These are good questions for adults too.

Ask yourself, every time you feel uncomfortable, "Am I being me?", "How can I be me right now?" "What do I need and how can I give that to myself?"

30 Second Parenting Strategy
Complaining

Change the situation, leave the situation, or accept it.
All else is madness.

-Eckhart Tolle

That statement bears repeating.

We complain to try to change something and/or to try to get what we want, as a means to get something that we think will make us happy.

The opposite is true, according to Eckhart Tolle: "Complaining cements the ego." Eckhart explains that we don't know that complaining is really an attempt at showing a sense of superiority: "I'm right, I know how it should be done. I'm superior if I know." Those thoughts come from the ego/identities and cause upsets.

Kids learn complaining from us.

Many people never realize that complaining doesn't change anything, even after many years of it.

If you stop yourself when you are complaining and just get quiet, you will begin to experience peace more often. Notice how you feel inside when you complain; it's never truly good.

Other strategies to take you out of complaining are to remind yourself:

— I'm still alive.
— I don't know the big picture and that's okay.

— If I'm upset and complaining I'm not in alignment with Divinity, I'm in alignment with my own beliefs.
— I don't want to cement the ego and cause myself more misery.
— I am not superior.
— My ego wants me to think I'm right.
— Complaining will not change anything.
— Complaining doesn't feel good – ever.

30 Second Parenting Strategy
"A Secret Message" To Yourself

Self-regulation is possible.

Deep rhythmic breathing changes our level of consciousness because the breath is what connects us to life. It gives us life. No breath, no life. Notice when you give all of your attention to your breathing, you can't think (as taught by Eckhart Tolle). The mind takes a break. When the mind isn't being used, our operating system is consciousness itself.

Deep breathing activates our natural relaxation response because the mind isn't in the way.

Deep breathing gets oxygen in the brain to help it work better.

Breath work is an ancient and popular method among the Masters' because it's our link to life. They teach that controlled breath brings more balance to the body, mind, thoughts, and emotions.

Some masters teach that slower breathing leads to a longer life.

When a child is upset, ask them to take slow deep breaths; in through the nose and out through the nose until they feel calm.

According to an article on kidsrelaxation.com, when teaching kids, it's helpful to tell them that "deep breathing is a secret message that tells the body and mind to relax."

Teach kids deep breathing exercises when they are calm, so they can use them more efficiently when they feel an upset begin. Do the same for yourself.

Try it now and notice what happens to thinking and to your body.

30 Second Parenting Strategy
Whose Business is It?

"Get rich and keep your two cents to yourself."
-Guy Finley

Byron Katie teaches three kinds of business: God's business, the others' business, and my business.

If the word 'God' bothers you, use the word you like best: Creation, Source, Universal Intelligence, Divine Intelligence, Buddha Nature, Christ Consciousness, the Field, etc. As long as you refer to that which is greater than us, any word will do.

Examples of Creation's business: a storm, death, nature.

Examples of the other's business: their problems, their solutions, what they say, even if it's something about me. What they feel, think, perceive, and do.

Examples of my business: what I think, feel, perceive, and do.

When we are in the others' business or God's business; as Katie says, "Who's at home in our business?"

Divine Intelligence can't appear if we're not there (inside of ourselves).

We don't like anyone in our business unless we specifically ask them for help. It's harder for us to see that much of our time is spent in the other's business and we're stressed out because of it. Notice the 'advice-giver' in you. Maybe we don't know what the other needs. Maybe what we think is right for them isn't right for them. It's peaceful to stay quiet instead of jumping in with unasked for advice.

With younger children, notice when you're wanting to insert yourself into their business when it's unnecessary. Notice the peace of not inserting yourself.

With teenage children, stay in your business as much as you can, and, at the same time, talk to your child about their problems: "Would you talk to me? I'll listen."

Respecting that others have a life to live and that *their business is their own* goes a long way towards peaceful relationships.

30 Second Parenting Strategy
The Power of Observation

The ability to observe without evaluating
is the highest form of intelligence.
                                                    -J Krishnamurti

Pretend your child is someone else's and observe them throughout the week.

Observe, in this case, means:

— Watch them, without giving your opinion to them.
— Pay attention, be present, to what is actually happening.
— Study them with curiosity.
— Pretend you are writing an article on them and want to make sure you capture everything about them.

What did you notice about them?

What did you notice about you?

This simple exercise will give you valuable insight into your children and yourself. You will begin to notice the real needs of the child. You will also begin to notice your helpful and unhelpful thoughts, actions and words while relating to the child.

Observation brings transformative awareness.

30 Second Parenting Strategy
Every Moment is New

The end of boredom.

What does that mean? It means that when all expectations fall away, every moment feels new because it is new.

Sages, mystics, visionaries, awakened human beings, and self-realized people talk about this as a way of existence; every moment is new even if you are doing the same thing you did yesterday.

My granddaughter, Lily, at age 2 ½ taught me something about this. She was standing up on the kitchen chair, so she could see the "reindeer" out the window. There were three white-tailed deer grazing near the trees at the back of the property. She stood up three different times to look at them and each time she did, she exclaimed, "Look, Grama, there are reindeer!" She was as excited the last time as she was the first two times.

I wondered what I was missing. The first time I looked at the deer, I was excited. The second time, I was a little less excited. The third time I glanced at them, but my attention was drawn to Lily. Her excitement and innocence were genuine. It was like seeing the deer was new to her each time.

Sadhguru teaches that right now is the only time it will ever be this moment. In that way, everything is new. It is (month, day, time) and it will never be that time again.

The ancients teach that the river is always changing and every time you step foot in it, it's changed. It's never the same river:

Heraclitis, a Greek Philosopher stated: "No man ever steps in the same river twice, for it's not the same river and he's not the same man."

Our bodies are always creating new cells and destroying old ones. Therefore, we are new in each moment. In the same way, time is acting on everything we set our senses on and all of it is constantly changing. Change truly is the only constant. It's always happening, so everything is always new.

I thought back to the times I experienced Presence, and in that case, everything felt new. I wondered why each time I saw the deer, it didn't feel new. That led to this exercise:

Take a minute now to look around you and tell yourself that what you are seeing is new – because this moment is new. This helps us shift our perspective to the peacefulness of now.

Several times a day, remind yourself to look at things through these new eyes and see what happens.

30 Second Parenting Strategy
Parents Who Fight

Fighting never solves a problem, but it always creates one.

If your kids know you are fighting with your partner, this is what they'd like to say to you:

> Dear Mom and Dad,
>
> When you know I've heard you argue, please tell me: that I'm okay, that you'll help each other work out the problem honestly so each person's needs are honored, that you won't take it out on me, that you will say sorry when you are wrong (and if you are fighting you are wrong). Please assure me that I don't have to pick sides, or, be scared of you.
>
> If you do this, I will be able to be a responsible and honest adult about my own arguments with another person.
>
> Please learn to do this so you can teach me.
>
> Love, your child.

30 Second Parenting Strategy
Helping Each Other (Instead of Hindering)

When we learn this, we give up fighting.

Amanda, my daughter, used an upset with her kids to teach them this strategy: helping is more fun than hurting.

One wanted to do a handstand using the couch for support so she asked her mom and sister, who were in her way, to please move so she could. Amanda said she'd be happy to move for her, but her sister stayed on the couch, moving only a bit. When she did the handstand, she, of course, kicked her sister, who hadn't really moved out of the way. Her sister then kicked her back.

Amanda invited each of them to remember a time when they helped each other and remember how that felt.

Then, when Amanda used the opportunity to look into what her daughter was resisting by not moving away from the couch, she discovered that her daughter didn't want to feel that someone was better than her, so she stopped her sister from doing the handstand. She felt she wasn't good enough. That could be dealt with!

If you can, give everyone what they want. The reason we don't is because we have a fear that we might miss out, be shown up, not matter, or lose something.

Byron Katie demonstrates this in an interesting way. She says if someone you think you love wants to leave you, give them roller blades (so they can get away faster!). Why would we want someone who doesn't want us? Help them go. It will be better for us in the end.

Remind yourself that giving the other what they want (when we can) is 'saying yes to life' (as taught by Byron Katie) and that whatever we fear we'll lose is likely not ours or is unnecessary to our true deep inner happiness.

The next time someone asks something of you, see if you can give it, and feel the difference between that and resisting 'on painful principle'.

30 Second Parenting Strategy
"What can I do to help?"

Help your brother's boat across,
and your own will reach the shore.

-Hindu Proverb

When it felt like my world was crashing down around me, and I was sitting on the back step, crying, my oldest brother, Ken, came and sat down beside me and asked, "What can I do to help?" He didn't even ask me what was wrong. There was no judgment, no advice, and the pressure I felt inside faded into gratitude for him.

Sometimes those words, themselves, do the healing.

Over many years, as I applied this strategy, a bonus appeared: the more we give the more fulfilled we feel.

Give others what they need, not what we think we need. That was another part of the lesson he taught me that day. Even though I did tell him what happened later in our conversation, before he knew, he was willing to help however I needed it.

30 Second Parenting Strategy
Indecision and Confusion

Mind.
A beautiful servant.
A dangerous master.

-Osho

Indecision comes from being confused. Confusion comes from not having/liking all the facts, and from relying on thoughts that aren't always reliable.

Slowing down any situation helps slow down the mind's false assumptions, conclusions, and expectations.

Until we can see what's really going on, we are blocking clarity. Thinking we know what is going on without some reflection is akin to regurgitating all the wrongs of the past and imprinting them on the current situation.

I used to co-own a day care and have an example from those days: let's say you have paid a lot of money for a daycare, but they have a rule that you cannot bring your child when they have a fever. If your child has a fever one day and no one is around to help you with childcare, the mind can stick on a useless thought such as the fact that you pay a lot of money for the service. Those types of thoughts keep you from practical thinking and practical action. In the example given, time will be spent in frustration and non-productivity (which is what happens when we are confused).

Here is an example of slowing down our thinking during an upset:

The day care won't take my child because of his/her fever.
I paid a lot of money for the day care. (The mind distracts with false defenses).
They should change. (The mind runs other people's businesses and is in an extreme state of confusion).
I don't know what to do. (The mind thinks it knows everything and also thinks it doesn't know anything).
They should change. (The mind repeats itself).
(Notice when the mind stays focussed on the negative - and then slow down your thinking – that will take it out of the no-exit loop of unhappily 'going nowhere' fast).
I have to work. (Fact).
I need help. (Fact).
Who can help in this situation? (Practical questioning).

You can see that putting attention on what you can't change won't help your situation.

Instead of listening to the rambling complaints of the mind, ask yourself this:

What can I do that works for everyone – what's practical? Get quiet when you ask the question and wait, with curiosity.

This is what the mind is supposed to be used for.

This seems simple and it is. When you 'checkmate your mind,' it's meanderings have to cease. Other than that, the mind is chattering based on beliefs learned as a child; in this case the belief could be something like, "If I pay good money, I should get what I want."

Don't let thoughts carry you away into confusion.

30 Second Parenting Strategy
Apologizing

It won't kill you. It'll just feel like it.

Sometimes we think we don't have to apologize to kids for our poor behavior. We'd be wrong to think that way.

When we are conscious enough to apologize, kids are usually pretty quick to forgive. That's because forgiveness is natural.

A genuine apology includes:

— saying we're sorry,
— seeing how we can make it up to the other,
— doing our own inner work on our behavior, words, or actions.

I've noticed with my own parenting that 'as the one in charge' I require that the kids take responsibility for their behavior, but I don't always take responsibility for mine. I just call myself 'right' and forget that snapping at them *isn't* right. It doesn't feel right inside of me and it doesn't feel right to the kids.

If I think I'm upset about something they've done, I'm wrong. I'm upset because of something I'm believing, not because they've done something wrong. It's my job to bring myself back to my True Nature without blaming them. Even if their words or actions don't serve, my upsetting judgment will always make it worse, not better, and that's no reason for *me* to be negative.

The other acting out is never a good reason for me to.

For example, if the child acts out and hits another child and I get upset with the child and reprimand them in a loud, scary voice, I'm responsible for my behavior. It is possible to guide them without a loud, scary voice. It's also much more peaceful for everyone. It is a guarantee that I will have regret for my behavior, and it always helps if I truly apologize.

Make your life easier and apologize when you mess up and do what it takes to make it right.

If you have trouble apologizing because you don't want to admit what you've done (you think it makes you bad), then use Blessing Mistakes on yourself: "I matter so much more than this mistake of not apologizing." After you give yourself some relief, it will be easier to apologize. To be clear, Blessing Mistakes has a part two: making it right. This is to help you get all the way free of a mistake.

30 Second Parenting Strategy
Harm

If you can, help others; if you cannot do that, at least do not harm them. Dalai Lama XIV

The Buddha taught that if what you are going to do will harm someone, don't do it.

The person we harm, begins to think harming themselves and others is okay. The whole world is acting this out.

Every time we harm another, we are harming ourselves.

Stop and notice you don't feel good inside in the exact moment you are harming someone else.

We don't appear to notice this because the level of consciousness we are operating at while we are harming the other is righteousness. I'm right and they deserve it. At that level of consciousness, we don't notice how out of balance we feel inside while we are harming the other. It always shows up after with internal struggle, talking to ourselves in our head for hours, days, years after the incident about how right we were and how wrong the other is. Notice that's not a pleasant state to be in.

Bringing understanding to an upset is the only thing that will change it long-term. Harming someone because we're upset won't help – ever.

Notice when you are about to hurt another human being and know that it comes from a part of you that only knows how to cause and feel pain. Ask yourself if that's what you want.

30 Second Parenting Strategy
Remorse

Remorse taught me love.

My Jungian Dream Analyst told me a story that succinctly defines the depth and healing capacity of expressing true remorse without accusing or blaming anyone else.

The United Nations had a committee trying to restore good relations in South Africa after Apartheid. A man who had been ordered to set up and kill another man told his story; the depth of his remorse could be heard in his voice. The mother of the man he killed sat in front of him. She told her story; how heart-wrenching it was to have her child killed. The depth of her pain could be heard in her voice. They were instructed to speak only of their own experience, to make sure they didn't blame. At the end, at the same time, the man said, "Forgive me, my mother," and the mother of the man who was killed, said, "Forgive me, my son." The members of the committee who watched were stunned. Neither the man nor the woman knew what the other was saying. They spoke different dialects.

True remorse gets us in touch with the deep sorrow we all carry. Honest remorse doesn't blame life or others, it only names what the feelings are and that is freeing.

Explain to the other what your experience is without ever blaming them. Blame has never, and will never, solve any problem. Expressing your pain will bring the other to their natural state: humanitarianism.

30 Second Parenting Strategy
I Am My Mother/I Am My Father

*"The greatest burden a child must bear
is the unlived life of its parents."*

Carl Jung

We are part of our parents. Their DNA is in us. Their beliefs are in us.

Repeating our parents' behaviors and patterns is unavoidable, just as repeating their DNA is unavoidable - until we bring awareness to our beliefs and the behaviors they cause.

If you want to live your own life to the best of your ability, and, want to parent from your True Nature without subconscious beliefs unknowingly adopted from your parents, make a list of ways in which your parents parented you and see how you are like them.

Seeing and feeling how you are alike is enough to bring you into awareness and that's enough to begin to change it.

Don't listen to yourself when you hear yourself say, "I am not like them at all." The mind WILL say that to you as you read this.

Just get this job done so you can set yourself free to be yourself. If our parents passed down genes that predisposed you to diabetes, you'd want to free yourself of diabetes if you could. Of course, you'd like to free yourself of their beliefs; the ones that have unknowingly become your own.

Follow the simple instructions below to free yourself of beliefs that don't serve and fall back into the state of love, even with people who abused or abandoned you. Why should you suffer any longer if someone hurt you?

During a similar exercise in a class I was teaching, with a man (whose mother tried to kill him), he said, "I will do this, but I want you and everyone here to know that I hate my mother, and nothing will change that." At the end of the exercise, which took about an hour, he said, "I don't know what happened, but I feel love, even when I think of her." That doesn't mean he needs to go to her (she may still be crazy) but it does mean that he was able to set himself free of painful behaviors that were similar to his mother that we causing him to hate. When we hate, we hurt. Hating anyone who hurt us hurts us more.

To free yourself of behaviors that are similar to your mother's:

I am my mother

She's _____ (state one negative behavior/ trait/characteristic with regard to her parenting. It's okay if she's not alive, do it anyway).

I am just like her in that way, and here's how:_____ (sit quietly and let the mind show you with an image or words how you are exactly like her as a parent).

Feel all the feelings (physical and emotional) until they pass.

Repeat the exercise at least 10 times, using different behaviors each time until you feel at peace with your mother.

Do the same for your father.

Here are some examples:

I am my mother.

She left me.
How am I just like her?
I left my children when I didn't give them enough attention.

She was addicted, and it affected me.
How am I just like her?
I am addicted and it affects my children.

She was self-centered and could only think of herself, not of how her actions were affecting the lives of her children.
How am I just like her?
I am self-centered as a parent and put my business life before my kids and that affected the lives of my children.

I am my father.

He didn't let me speak.
How am I just like him?
I interrupted my children and didn't let them speak, and I talk too much instead of listening.

He lived under the rule that he made all the rules.
How am I just like him?
Sometimes, I still believe I make the rules. I dictate to others how they should talk to me.

Ugh.

As the truth surfaces, the painful beliefs are felt and then they dissolve, leaving us feeling natural.

30 Second Parenting Strategy
Conscious Parenting in The Tween and Teen years

Rather than clamping down harder on your kids when they begin to discover their own autonomy, Dr. Shefali advises a surrender of control. Begin to trust in your own parenting up until the teen years and that the kids will work it out.

To put this into practice: notice when you want to control your child, and imagine that you can safely "loosen the reins," as Dr. Shefali says.

It's inevitable that kids are going to get themselves into situations that have consequences. It's nice for you (and them) if you can be calm when they do.

Ask the question often, "Can I loosen the reins?" This will benefit you and your child.

The result: more peace, less stress, better relationships with kids.

30 Second Parenting Strategy
How Can We Make This Work for Both of Us?

The best side to be on
is everyone's.

Many of us think that avoiding conflict is solving conflict. That strategy just keeps conflict alive long after it could have been resolved.

When an upset with another happens, one excellent strategy, rather than blaming or arguing is to ask, "How can we make this work for both of us?" as taught by self-care expert, Suzi Lula.

It is natural for us to want to support others.

It is unnatural for us to fight tooth and nail to get what we want at the expense of another. It goes against the natural compassion and inclusiveness we have inside of us.

This is really useful in the 'tween' and teen years. It's also a peaceful relationship saver when used with other adults.

30 Second Parenting Strategy
Teenage Rebellion and Authority

When your children are teenagers, it's important to have
a dog so that someone in the house is happy to see you.
-Nora Ephron

Parents are seen by children as authority figures. When authority figures are abusive, verbally, or physically, then rebellion is not far behind.

It seems natural to rebel against abuse.

When a parent criticizes a child, the child wants to rebel against that because they don't want to be considered 'bad'.

If we experienced abusive parents, we grow up unconsciously deciding to disrespect authority. That will be painful for us because authority is just authority. Disrespect is its own issue to be resolved.

We all believe that abuse should not be tolerated.

In some ways, the other can't help themselves when they are abusing; they are identified and can only operate from that level of consciousness.

It is not easy for parents to admit that they are abusive, but it's courageous to be honest. Even if we don't hit our kids, we do abuse them emotionally or mentally at times.

Criticizing a child or another is abusive. We know this because we feel abused by someone who criticizes us. Nobody likes to be criticized.

Sadly, we believe that we can abuse others with judgment and condemnation, while demanding that they can't do that to us.

I can abuse you, but you can't abuse me. I can criticize you, but you can't criticize me. I can judge you, but you can't judge me.

While we are busy criticizing (abusing) our kids, we are also insisting that they respect us.

That means we are teaching our children to be nice to their abusers. We want them to be nice to us while we go one criticizing them. This sets them up to attract a partner later who will abuse them.

Kids need correction, not criticism. Correction comes without judgment and big emotions. Correction comes with compassion. It mostly involves getting the child to reconnect with themselves and with Creation.

Remember how smart we thought we were as young adults when we disrespected our parents, even only in our minds? We all think we know more than our parents.

It seems like a good idea to disrespect authority that abuses, BUT will that solve the problem of authorities abusing power? It never has and never will.

As we grow older, this belief, 'IT'S SMART TO DISRESPECT AUTHORITY (because they abuse),' is at war with the belief 'I have to be nice to my abuser'.

We will NEED to see authorities as abusive if this was our experience as children. We will also NEED to be nice to abusers if this was our experience as children. We will also want to rebel. What a mess.

These beliefs permeate our relationships with others. If we see others as authority figures, we mechanically default to disrespecting them *and* trying to please them. Think of being pulled over by a police officer and being nice and polite, completely deferring to them, and, at the same time, cursing them under our breath. This is disrespecting and being nice to authority at the same time.

If we see men as an authority, we must disrespect them. If we see women as the authority, we must disrespect them.

In men's and women's relationships, you can see how this can cause war on a day-to-day basis. If one takes the lead and is critical, the other will rebel and that will cause trouble. There is no solution available, there is only a continuing cycle of viewing events through eyes that can only see that authority should be rebelled against.

Think of your siblings/parents/relatives. Who is the abusive authority you disrespect? Your mind has made them your authority. Your mind has decided to rebel.

There is another way.

What will help is to begin to see where you abuse/punish, judge, criticize or control your children, or others, and stop yourself. It's not always possible to stop ourselves in the moment, but it's always possible to notice when we've done it. That's enough to begin to change it. To make it easier on yourself, Bless your mistake of abusing, judging, criticizing or controlling your child and then make it right.

Another reason kid's rebel is when they feel too controlled. Let them experience life. Let them make mistakes. (You know how to Bless them). "Loosen the reins." Let them experience falling down. They're going to anyway; we can't stop that. When they have some freedom and take the lead, the need for rebellion subsides.

This is as much for you as it is for the child. When we "loosen the reins," (as Dr. Shefali suggests) we all feel less stress. It's *very* stressful to control someone all the time. Remember what Rainer Rilke said, The child has a life and it's being lived. It is their life.

30 Second Parenting Strategy
I Have A Problem

*How come know-it-all's don't know
how annoying they are?*

After I had been teaching self-inquiry (how to go inside of ourselves and see the cause of stress), and conscious inner conflict resolution, for several years, my son, Cody, taught me a valuable lesson even though he was 23 years old at the time. Our kids don't stop teaching us just because they grow older.

He and I were having lunch together, a rare treat because he lives several hours away. He said, "Mom, I have a problem." He then went on to describe his problem in a few simple sentences.

Since I am his mom, and was a teacher of conflict resolution, I thought I had the answer to his problem. I said, "Cody would you like to do the work?" That meant using the techniques I had learned, taught, and used myself.

He said, "Mom, you didn't hear me. I said I have a problem."

I had to pause and consider what he was telling me. I thought I had understood him and responded appropriately, but when I thought about it a bit more, I decided on a different tactic. "Cody, I hear you telling me you have a problem. If you would like help with it, you can ask me." More blah, blah from me.

He said, "Mom, you didn't hear me. I said I have a problem."

Oh, no. I'm supposed to know how to handle these situations. I don't want to fail as a mom. My son has a problem. I *need* to help. I teach the healing nature of conflict. I wanted him to use the conflict to heal himself. I didn't quite know what to say, so I put my sandwich down, and thought some more and finally it came to me and I said, "Cody, you have a problem."

He said, "Thank you mom. It's my problem."

He never asked for help, he was just sharing that he had a problem. I jumped in as the fixer of all problems. He can solve his problems in any way he sees fit. It's his problem. What a relief for both of us.

It's very stressful to adopt the role of a 'problem-fixer' because we can't fix the other's problems. We can hardly fix our own. We don't know that the best problem solver is to be connected, so the problems appear as secondary, and the people appear as most important.

We don't need to fix the other. I repeat that to myself whenever I get the notion that I should 'help' them without them asking.

There is a turning point as a parent where you let go of the reins completely, and remain in support of whatever they do, no matter what it is. This may sound strange because we don't want to support a young child with a problem, or an adult child with an alcohol problem, a shopping addiction, or any other problem, do we? Yes, we do. We extricate ourselves from their problem (Guy Finley's 'Making Peace with Problems') and support them by loving them and doing whatever else will serve to demonstrate love. This is true for anyone we are in relationship with.

When kids are young, we guide and correct them, while teaching them connection. As they grow up, we slowly let them take over their problems. The next generation, as is always true, is more advanced and likely wiser than this one.

30 Second Parenting Strategy
Adversity

The invitation to inner wisdom.

Since it's unavoidable, teach your kids that adversity cultivates us, helps us dig deep inside, and draws out our pure intelligence, creativity, and compassion.

If you don't teach your kids that adversity happens, and how to deal with it, they will adopt a victim mentality.

> "Victims are the most violent people on the planet."
> Byron Katie

That quotation means that when we believe we are victims, we will want to lash out.

As I was walking through a market in Mexico one day, I saw a vendor talking to a small group of people huddled around her table. She was pointing to a statue on the table and explaining how she makes them out of clay found in the mountains nearby. The statue appeared odd to me at first. It was of a woman's head. The head was sitting in a boat and there were fish scattered about representing the few friends willing to travel through hard times with her. Around the woman's forehead sat a thorn of crowns representing adversity that is inescapable in each of our lives. On the very top of her head, a position requiring a great deal of grace to maintain, were three tiny birds in a nest representing trauma.

Adversity can be carried gracefully, or it can be worn like a painful 'crown of thorns'. Traumas take a few minutes and transform either to opportunity, or to a stress-causing story that drags out UNNECESSARY AND UNNATURAL suffering for years.

Close your eyes and think of a traumatic moment in your life. How long did it last? See if you can see the 'silver lining' in that particular cloud. How did it positively change you? Why did it help you grow? What did you learn?

How trauma affects us long-term is up to us.

Next time you look at your child, remember that they are their own support system because of their connection to Divine Intelligence. Adversity helps to draw their attention to the Divinity inside of themselves.

Know that your children are counting on you to look at them in this way. Let them come up with ways to solve their own problems.

30 Second Parenting Strategy
Reality 'Shots'

A picture _is_ worth a thousand words.

When we grow up, we can often look back at our childhood and tend to remember, focus on, and then obsess over the trauma's or upsets we experienced. We can forget that much of the time during our childhood we don't even remember; in those times we were Present so there is nothing to remember.

Once when I was looking through old family black and white photos, I began to realize that my childhood, while it had some big bumps, it also held good times.

As I looked at these pictures, I felt a subtle change overtake me. It felt like a balancing. I was seeing the good right there in front of me, in black and white. My mind had been trying to convince me for a long time that I should hang on to that painful childhood I remembered. My heart saw the uselessness of that strategy. I just wanted proof that I was a victim. That didn't help me in any way.

I thought this might help my kids, so the next time they came home, I dug out their childhood pictures, and, as they went through them, I could see the looks on their faces start to reflect the softness inside of them, brought out by the 'good times' depicted in the pictures.

30 Second Parenting Strategy
Happy Family Tips to Reduce Stress

Happiness is natural. Uncover yours!

Bruce Feiler, author of the *New York Times* bestseller, *The Secrets of Happy Families* asked himself how he could make his family happier. He asked families, scholars, Warren Buffet's bankers, Green Berets, and other experts.

Some of the strategies he found to "cut parental screaming in half," are:

— reduce stress with kids by having checklists for daily living because it teaches accountability and kids love to check off their contributions.

— have weekly 20-minute family meetings and let the kids have input using these questions:
  o what worked well this week?
  o what didn't work well this week?
  o what do we agree to work on this week?

— have a family meal or snack together, even if it's only 10 minutes, and let the kids do the most talking. Research shows that this strategy means kids are less likely to drink, smoke, do drugs, get pregnant, commit suicide, or develop eating disorders.

— keep a family history and share stories with your kids (both positive and negative ones.) Kids who know their history have a greater sense for the scope of life and increased emotional stability.

— empower your children: enlist your children with problem solving; plan their own goals, set schedules, and let them make mistakes.

— preserve the core and stimulate progress: define your mission and identify the family mission statement: have a p.j. party and decide what's important. Ask this question: "What do we want to be?" and let everyone participates in the answers. If one of your statements is, "We want to have fun together," this statement will remind you to make sure you arrange time together to have fun.

— adapt all the time.

— learn how to argue (learn how to communicate without big emotions): separate the kids into different spaces so everyone has cool-down time, ask everyone to come up with three alternatives, and bring everyone back together.

— use this "FBI Hostage Negotiation" strategy:

   o active listening: listen without interrupting; when they finish, ask some questions if you need clarity on their point of view. You will always learn something if you are open.

   o empathy: you understand where they're coming from and how they feel.

   o rapport: now that you listened, they can begin to trust you.

   o influence: now that you've earned their trust, you can problem-solve with them and recommend a course of action.

   o behavioral change: the child acts and maybe does something different as a result of this strategy.

Contact Bruce: https://www.brucefeiler.com

30 Second Parenting Strategy
Understanding Stress with Sadhguru

Stress, let's break up.

"You get stressful because you do not know how to handle your mind, your emotions, your body, your energies, your system."

"Stress is a natural outcome of unconscious living."

He teaches a simple yoga technique called Inner Engineering (part of it can be taken online) and Shambhavi, (taught online and in many cities in the world) a short, daily practice that brings about tremendous physical healing and naturally joyful states.

"Do Inner Engineering for 21 minutes a day and take your pulse rate before and after food, for six weeks, check your pulse rate and see it will be considerably down...The lowering of the pulse indicates that your system is going at an easier pace, that means it's going much more efficiently."

For me, this system has increased my own natural joy in addition to helping me physically. I used to require a visit to the chiropractor once a week for most of my adult life due to an injury when I was young, my feet and hips hurt, and I had frequent neck-related headaches. That's all gone!

More importantly, as Sadhguru says, "Sadhana" (daily spiritual or yoga practice) is an invitation to the Divine." That means peace awaits all of us who use any means to become Present.

https://www.youtube.com/watch?v=F23qjR9I9RE

Inner Engineering:

https://www.innerengineering.com/online

30 Second Parenting Strategy
Animals are Therapy

Animals are such agreeable friends—
they ask no questions; they pass no criticisms.
-George Eliot, British Author

Most children feel naturally joyful when an animal is present. Most adults do too.

They can be a lot of work and responsibility, but they give back to you the blessing of unconditional love, unless it's a cat, and then you give the love and learn about detachment!

If it works for you and you have the resources (time and money), they can bring a lot of goodness to a family.

30 Second Parenting Strategy
Upa Yoga for Kids (& Adults)

Yoga means union (Sadhguru)
Union means no uneasiness

Get your kids to do Upa Yoga with you in the morning or evening. It's too wonderful to even describe. Each yoga practice is relatively short and simple but yields great results.

It addresses physical problems, nightmares, sleep issues, fear, etc., etc., etc.

Google Sadhguru Upa Yoga app. The downloadable app that makes doing the yoga properly very easy.

30 Second Parenting Strategy
Fun Yoga for Kids

Learn through fun and you never want to stop!

Another kind of yoga is Cosmic Kids and is a really fun and great introduction to yoga, which will get them ready to move to Sadhguru's yoga as they get older.

Yoga is about unity, flexibility, strength and stillness in the mind and body. In those states, stress doesn't have a stronghold. That's why it's good to have children learn a daily practice when they are young.

Google this YouTube video created by Cosmic Kids that demonstrates a unique yoga program for kids that draws them in, entertains them, and gives them the benefits associated with yoga.

Tell everyone with kids about this website – they'll love you for it! http://www.cosmickids.com

This is a 3-minute video taken from a 23-minute yoga workout for kids:

https://www.youtube.com/watch?v=YR1OxBk8BF4

30 Second Parenting Strategy
Attention Deficit

Lots of attention helps attention deficit.

Just because they don't fit into the mold, doesn't mean they don't fit. We all fit. As parents, it's our job to help our kids feel like they fit and find where they do. Turn their attention towards things they like to do.

When we learn to put our attention on what is important, we become productive, connected, creative and joyful.

Kids who have attention deficit need connection so helping them find ways to feel connected will help them immensely.

The real help for attention-deficit kids is to give them your full attention. Observe them closely to see what triggers them. See if you can determine their real needs.

If they ADHD (Attention deficit hyperactive disorder), let them move around. Find creative ways for them to learn (jumping up and down on the couch while learning their spelling words, for example).

Find lots of things they love to do and let them do them.

Teach them meditation and yoga from Sadhguru's app or Cosmic Kids.

Kids who act out *will* have all of your attention. It may as well be productive attention.

Every day use all the upsets you have due to their experience, to grow yourself by using a self-inquiry strategy.

30 Second Parenting Strategy
Equality

How do we know everything and
everyone has a right to life?
Because they are here.

-Byron Katie

I am smart.
I am dumb.
I am old.
I am young.
I am black.
I am white.
I am brown.
I am rich.
I am poor.
I am gay.
I am heterosexual.
I am beautiful.
I am ugly.
I AM – Everyone is this – equal.

Most people claim to believe in equality, but few people live it.

Treat your children as your equals. They are.

Besides, we all made of the exact same stuff.

Our children may come into the world later than we do, but how could that make them less in any way?

Pretend you're talking to Divine Intelligence when you are talking to your child. You are.

Sadhguru advises us to not look up to anybody and not look down on anybody. That's what equality is.

30 Second Parenting Strategy
Autism

If a child cannot learn in the way we teach,
we must teach in a way the child can learn.
-Ole Ivar Lovaas, Ph.D.,
(world-renowned autism expert)

Children living along the autism spectrum have a great deal to teach humanity. They may even help us bring back humanity.

Osho teaches that we need to find where everyone fits. Sadhguru teaches that unless there is anger, there is no problem. People are born with different capabilities and a wise person would find where the child's capabilities lie and guide them in that direction. Living with children with high levels of autism can be extremely stressful if you are not at a higher level of awareness. The challenges can seem insurmountable.

The first action is to get everyone in the family what they need while keeping the child safe.

Observe everyone's needs, set up the home to accommodate the child and others as best as you can, and get family, community, and government support where possible. If you have a child living with autism, you already know this.

Don't mix up showing you care with the many practical actions you need to take. We can love and care about another human being but that doesn't mean we don't need to get our own needs met, especially if we care-give to others.

The course on Autism found at www.courserebel.com under Brenda Miller takes you through a number of freeing exercises. They are based on consciousness work; clearing obstacles in the mind so that love and humanitarianism can be our natural go-to.

30 Second Parenting Strategy
Traumatic Stress Release

It's traumatic to hold onto trauma.

Everyone has stress and has experienced trauma.

Sadhguru teaches that every touch, every sight, every sound, every experience that we have ever undergone is stored in the mind/body. With this understanding, imagine how much stress is stored in us.

One paradigm for stress release called TRE (Tension & Trauma Release Exercise), created by Dr. David Berceli, who worked with trauma victims in war-torn areas, is highly effective in releasing stored stress. It consists of a few simple stretches followed by initiated shaking to release deep-rooted stress, tension, and trauma. The shaking unwinds trapped tension and allows the body and mind to calm itself.

Animals naturally do this when they have a skirmish. Eckhart Tolle shares that ducks in the pond shake off the energy after a fight!

We have learned to suppress or override the natural response of shaking to release fear/trauma rather than to actively release it.

Intro to TRE: http://traumaprevention.com/home-video/

The Revolutionary Trauma Release Exercise

The MP4 download is available at: http://www.namastepublishing.com

The following video clip with Dr. Berceli changes one's level of awareness about trauma and stress. He says all species evolve due to trauma and stress, even though it's not something we voluntarily wish upon ourselves or others. Most lives, however, do not escape this, so perhaps another way of dealing with trauma will be helpful. He also shares his understanding of people like Mother Teresa, Martin Luther King, Jr., Ghandi, and Nelson Mandela going deeply into their suffering and coming out the other side of it with peaceful messages and a raised level of consciousness.

More information is available on You Tube or on Dr. Berceli's websites:

http://www.bercelifoundation.org/s/1340/aff_2_home.aspx
(information)

Another way to release stress instantly is to holler loudly after the trauma. My own experience of an unusual release of fear was taught to me by my son, Cody. I was driving along the highway in my little motorhome and an oilfield truck crossed the highway in front of me. It was a close call, and I was shaking hard. Cody happened to call me a minute or so after the incident and I told him what happened, and he said, "Oh, mom you've got too much energy in your system. Stop and holler really loud and you'll release the energy, and you'll feel better." I did it and felt better. It worked.

30 Second Parenting Strategy
Fun with Kids

It's built into all of us.

Ask the kids what they'd like to do. If you can do it with them, do it.

Google 'fun with kids'. There are hundreds of websites with cheap or free ideas to do with kids.

Here's what came up when I Googled it:

Zen Habits

1. Have a reading marathon.
2. Write stories together.
3. Play soccer.
4. Paint or draw.
5. Create a fort in your living room out of blankets or cardboard boxes.
6. Go on a hike.
7. Have a sunset picnic at a park or beach.

Play board games.

http://zenhabits.net/100-ways-to-have-fun-with-your-kids-for/

Pinterest, Fun Stuff for Kids

Make a bouncy ball, a harmonica, fun home experiments, giving a cranky kid a foot rub...

https://www.pinterest.com/pragmaticmom/fun-stuff-for-kids/

Fun at Home with Kids

Fun math projects, make your fizzy bath bomb...

http://www.funathomewithkids.com

StoryBots - $40 per year +/-

This is one of my favorites. The grandkids love to play this, and they ask me to do StoryBots almost every time they come over. It's a site that allows you to add your child's pictures and they become the star of the story.

It's child safe, educational, fun, and entertaining.

http://www.storybots.com

The end (of a lot of trouble).

The best thing a child can have is a conscious parent who can point them to their own True Nature.

Brenda

Sample Day: For A Conscious Parent
Goal: Wellbeing

This is a sample of what a conscious parent's day looks like. Make your own plan based on what brings you natural joy and peace.

Share your experiences and ask any questions on our Facebook Page: Conscious Parents, Conscious Kids, and Kid Code.

It may feel impossible to incorporate each of these into your day, but if you make some simple changes and use some of the ideas, you will begin to notice more peace in your family. Remembering that these strategies work because they are based on the truth about who we are and how we can best operate in the world. Each time you use one, you raise the level of consciousness in yourself, and by extension (through modelling and the higher energy frequency you operate at that helps entrain the other to it).

Upon Waking: palms together and thank Creation for being alive today. Keep the palms together until you feel the feeling of gratitude.

Inner Engineering Yoga: or whatever practice you have that stretches the body and is also an "invitation to the Divine." Same for kids.

Designated Mediation Time with Kids: when possible, same place, same time; designated quiet area in the house. Quiet time, watching thoughts come and go without getting attached, watching the breath, etc. It's also helpful to meditate in solitude daily. In your car works if that's all that's available.

Gratitude Time: a conscious person is in the natural state of gratitude much of the time. One way to keep our awareness on gratitude is to have a designated gratitude time where each person in the family genuinely expresses gratitude for something or someone in their day.

The evening meal can be a good time to do this because enough time has passed to have opportunities for gratitude.

Your Upsets: with each upset you experience, use one of the strategies until you feel calm. For the more difficult issues, call your 'Freedom Friend' (that's your bestie who is also doing this kind of work to bring themselves relief).

Your Kids Upsets: if you get upset when your kids are upset, that's the sign that you have something inside of you (a wound, a misperception) that needs attention. You can do it in the moment or later if you need to deal with the child.

Also, invite the child to use one of the strategies with your help.

Throughout the Day: a prayer to Creation. Some examples are:

— From Guy Finley: 'More of Thee, Less of Me'. This prayer is asking that Creation become the operating system in us vs. our identities or conditioned mind as the operating system.

Play Time with Kids: connect, be playing yourself, and make friends with your kids through play.

Kids Free Play Time/Quiet Time: we need it, they need it.

Time in Nature with Kids: a great place to let of steam and get re-balanced by doing nothing other than being there.

Throughout the Day: use and teach the Diverting to Divinity strategies.

Bedtime Ritual for Kids:

— Get them to focus on the breath going into and coming out of their body (this changes their level of consciousness to a higher and less stressed level).
— Ask them if they have any upsets they would like to work on and use the strategy they like best.
— Read a book based in consciousness, not one of the classics that are often scary tales that include violence.
      o Coming soon: Mr. Upalupagus's Secret Secrets is a bedtime (or anytime) story to help bring kids and their parents back into a natural state when they feel stressed out. Mr. Upalupagus is a wise young elephant who takes his little-bit rowdy, but lovable crew on outer adventures around the world only to discover something beautiful about their inner selves – every time!

— Kids: Palms together, eyes closed, thank Creation for this day.
— Parents (with the child): Palms together, eyes closed, thank Creation for this day, thank Creation for this child.

The Masters

The people I refer to that live/d without stress once they came into operating from their pure intelligence are listed here. They are also my beloved teachers. Their wisdom can uncover our own.

Byron Katie

"Byron Katie, founder of The Work, has one job: to teach people how to end their own suffering. As she guides people through the powerful process of inquiry, she calls The Work, they find that their stressful beliefs—about life, other people, or themselves—radically shift and their lives are changed forever. Based on Byron Katie's direct experience of how suffering is created and ended, The Work is an astonishingly simple process, accessible to people of all ages and backgrounds, and requires nothing more than a pen, paper, and an open mind."

http://thework.com/en/about-byron-katie

Guy Finley

"BEST-SELLING "LETTING GO" author Guy Finley's encouraging, and accessible message is one of the true bright lights in our world today. His ideas go straight to the heart of our most important personal and social issues — relationships, success, addiction, stress, peace, happiness, freedom — and lead the way to a higher life.

Finley is the acclaimed author of *The Secret of Letting Go*, *The Essential Laws of Fearless Living* and 35 other major works that have sold over a million copies in 18 languages worldwide. He is Director of Life of Learning Foundation, a Center for Spiritual Discovery in Merlin, Oregon, and the Foundation's popular Key Lesson e-mails are read each week by a hundred thousand subscribers in 142 countries. Finley's work is widely endorsed by doctors, business professionals, celebrities, and religious leaders of all denominations."

https://www.guyfinley.org/about/guy-finley

Sadhguru

"Sadhguru, a yogi and profound mystic of our times, is a visionary humanitarian and a prominent spiritual leader. A contemporary Guru, rooted as strongly in mundane and pragmatic matters as he is in inner experience and wisdom, Sadhguru works tirelessly towards the physical, mental, and spiritual well-being of all. His mastery of the mechanisms of life, an outcome of his profound experience of the Self, guides in exploring the subtler dimensions of life.

At home in loincloth as much as he is in blue jeans, barefoot through the mighty Himalayas, or straddling a BMW motorcycle on the expressway, Sadhguru is the most unusual mystic that one can encounter. Marking a clear departure from mere customs and rituals, Sadhguru's scientific methods for self-transformation are both direct and powerful. Belonging to no particular tradition, Sadhguru incorporates and presents what is most valid for the contemporary life from the yogic sciences.

Sadhguru speaks at some of the world's most prominent international leadership forums. In January 2007, he participated in four panels at the World Economic Forum and spoke on issues ranging from diplomacy and economic development, to education and the environment. In 2006, he addressed the World Economic Forum, the Tallberg Forum in Sweden, and the Australian Leadership Retreat. He has also served as a delegate to the United Nations Millennium Peace Summit and the World Peace Congress.

Sadhguru's vision and understanding of modern social and economic issues have led to interviews with BBC, Bloomberg, CNBC, CNN, and Newsweek International. His insights are regularly featured in India's leading national newspapers. A well-known public figure, he regularly draws crowds of more than 300,000 people for his public talks and "Satsang's" (group meditation)."

https://www.ishafoundation.org/Sadhguru

Mooji

"Mooji is a direct disciple of Sri Harilal Poonja, the renowned Advaita master, or Papaji, as his followers call him. In 1987, a chance meeting with a Christian mystic was to be a life-changing encounter for Mooji. It brought him, through prayer, into the direct experience of the Divine within. Within a short period, he experienced a radical shift in consciousness so profound that outwardly, he seemed, to many who knew him, to be an entirely different person. As his spiritual consciousness awakened, a deep inner transformation began which unfolded in the form of many miraculous experiences and mystical insights. He felt a strong wind of change blowing through his life which brought with it a deep urge to surrender completely to divine will. Shortly after, he stopped teaching, left his home and began a life of quiet simplicity and surrender to the will of God as it manifested spontaneously within him. A great peace entered his being, and, has remained ever since."

https://mooji.org/biography/

Eckhart Tolle

"Eckhart is a spiritual teacher and author who was born in Germany and educated at the Universities of London and Cambridge. At the age of 29, a profound inner transformation radically changed the course of his life. The next few years were devoted to understanding, integrating, and deepening that transformation, which marked the beginning of an intense inward journey. Later, he began to work in London with individuals and small groups as a counselor and spiritual teacher. Eckhart shares his time between British Columbia, Canada, and California. Eckhart Tolle is the author of the #1 *New York Times* bestseller *The Power of Now* (translated into 33 languages) and the highly acclaimed follow-up A *New Earth*, which are widely regarded as two of the most influential spiritual books of our time.

Eckhart's profound yet simple teachings have already helped countless people throughout the world find inner peace and greater fulfillment in their lives. At the core of the teachings lies the transformation of consciousness, a spiritual awakening that he sees as the next step in human evolution. An essential aspect of this awakening consists in transcending our ego-based state of consciousness. This is a prerequisite not only for personal happiness but also for the ending of violence on our planet."

https://www.eckharttolle.com/about/

Adyashanti

"Adyashanti, author of *The Way of Liberation, Falling into Grace, True Meditation,* and *The End of Your World,* is an American-born spiritual teacher devoted to serving the awakening of all beings. His teachings are an open invitation to stop, inquire, and recognize what is true and liberating at the core of all existence.

Asked to teach in 1996 by his Zen teacher of 14 years, Adyashanti offers teachings that are free of any tradition or ideology. "The Truth I point to is not confined within any religious point of view, belief system, or doctrine, but is open to all and found within all."

Based in California, Adyashanti lives with his wife, Mukti, Associate Teacher of Open Gate Sangha. He teaches throughout North America and Europe, offering satsangs, weekend intensives, silent retreats, and a live internet radio broadcast.

"Adyashanti" means primordial peace."

https://www.adyashanti.org/index.php?file=aboutus

The Dalai Lama

"His Holiness the Dalai Lama is a man of peace. In 1989 he was awarded the Nobel Peace Prize for his non-violent struggle for the liberation of Tibet.

He has consistently advocated policies of non-violence, even in the face of extreme aggression. He also became the first Nobel Laureate to be recognized for his concern for global environmental problems.

His Holiness has travelled to more than 67 countries spanning 6 continents. He has received over 150 awards, honorary doctorates, prizes, etc., in recognition of his message of peace, non-violence, inter-religious understanding, universal responsibility and compassion. He has also authored or co-authored more than 110 books.

His Holiness has held discussions with heads of different religions and participated in many events promoting inter-religious harmony and understanding.

Since the mid-1980s, His Holiness has engaged in a dialogue with modern scientists, mainly in the fields of psychology, neurobiology, quantum physics and cosmology. This has led to a historic collaboration between Buddhist monks and world-renowned scientists in trying to help individuals achieve peace of mind. It has also resulted in the addition of modern science to the traditional curriculum of Tibetan monastic institutions re-established in exile."

https://www.dalailama.com/the-dalai-lama/biography-and-daily-life/brief-biography

Vernon Howard

"Vernon Howard was born in Haverhill, Massachusetts on March 16, 1918. When he was a boy his family moved to California where he lived for many years. He began writing and lecturing there on spiritual and psychological topics. He eventually moved from Los Angeles to Boulder City, Nevada where he lived and taught for many years. In 1979 he founded New Life Church and Literary Foundation.

From 1965 until his death in 1992 he wrote books and conducted classes which reflect a degree of skill and understanding that may be unsurpassed in modern history. Human Behavior Magazine once said of him, "Vernon Howard is probably the clearest writer on these subjects in the English language."

His warmth and refreshing sense of humor made him a delightful subject for interviews, talk shows and articles. In 1983 Michael Benner of station KLOS in Los Angeles, California said, "Vernon Howard is one of the most powerful speakers I have ever interviewed. He has an uncanny ability to cut through the fluff and puff and jolt people into seeing who they really are. At times humorous and gentle, at other times demanding and forceful, Vernon Howard holds the record for generating responses to our KLOS talk shows. Not everyone likes his message, but I can't imagine anyone turning him off."

Vernon Howard broke through to another world. He saw through the illusion of suffering and fear and loneliness. In The Esoteric Path to a New Life MP3 CD there is a marvelous interview with Vernon Howard. Also included in this album is the booklet of the same name which will give any new student a great introduction to Vernon Howard's works.

Today more than 8 million readers worldwide enjoy his exceptionally clear and inspiring presentations of the great truths of the ages.

Libraries, bookstores, health food stores and church bookshops all over the country sell Vernon Howard books, booklets, CDs, DVDs, MP3 CDs and much more. His material is widely used by doctors, psychiatrists, psychologists, clergymen, counselors, educators and people from all walks of life.

All his teachings center around one grand theme: ***"There is a way out of the human problem, and anyone can find it."***

http://www.anewlife.org/About/Vernon_Howard/vernon_howard.html

Osho

"Osho defies categorization. His thousands of talks cover everything from the individual quest for meaning to the most urgent social and political issues facing society today.

Osho's books are not written but are transcribed from audio and video recordings of his extemporaneous talks to international audiences. As he puts it, "So remember: whatever I am saying is not just for you... I am talking also for the future generations." Osho has been described by the Sunday Times in London as one of the "1000 Makers of the 20th Century" and by American author Tom Robbins as "the most dangerous man since Jesus Christ." Sunday Mid-Day (India) has selected Osho as one of ten people – along with Gandhi, Nehru and Buddha – who have changed the destiny of India. About his own work Osho has said that he is helping to create the conditions for the birth of a new kind of human being. He often characterizes this new human being as "Zorba the Buddha" – capable both of enjoying the earthy pleasures of a Zorba the Greek and the silent serenity of a Gautama the Buddha. Running like a thread through all aspects of Osho's talks and meditations is a vision that encompasses both the timeless wisdom of all ages past and the highest potential of today's (and tomorrow's) science and technology.

Osho is known for his revolutionary contribution to the science of inner transformation, with an approach to meditation that acknowledges the accelerated pace of contemporary life. His unique OSHO Active Meditations are designed to first release the accumulated stresses of body and mind, so that it is then easier to take an experience of stillness and thought-free relaxation into daily life."

https://www.osho.com/read/osho/about-osho

John de Ruiter

"Meetings with John are for the realization of meaning in all aspects of our existence, to address life by knowledge and sincerity rather than fear, desire, and speculation. Life is mysterious, but we are able to know. We know how we are being inside, when the heart is hard and when it is soft. We know kindness and love. We know what is true within and we can know the deeper meaning of this life.

Established by Canadian philosopher, John de Ruiter, this project is a direct engagement with reality. John holds regular meetings exploring, through dialogue and silent connection, the foundations and subtleties of being alive. The objective is existence calling attention to itself, compelling us to know and be what is true. The method is the only one that works: knowing and core-splitting honesty. "Core-splitting honesty simply wants to know the entire truth just so it can surrender to it and be it."

https://johnderuiter.com/about/

Alan Watts

"A prolific author and speaker, Alan Watts was one of the first to interpret Eastern wisdom for a Western audience. Born outside London in 1915, he discovered the nearby Buddhist Lodge at a young age. After moving to the United States in 1938, Alan became an Episcopal priest for a time, and then relocated to Millbrook, New York, where he wrote his pivotal book _The Wisdom of Insecurity: A Message for an Age of Anxiety_. In 1951 he moved to San Francisco where he began teaching Buddhist studies, and in 1956 began his popular radio show, "Way Beyond the West." By the early sixties, Alan's radio talks aired nationally, and the counterculture movement adopted him as a spiritual spokesperson. He wrote and traveled regularly until his passing in 1973."

http://www.alanwatts.org/life-of-alan-watts/

Yogananda

"Paramahansa Yogananda (1893–1952) is considered one of the preeminent spiritual figures of modern times.

Author of the best-selling spiritual classic _Autobiography of a Yogi_, this beloved world teacher came to America in 1920 from his native India, and was the first great master of yoga to live and teach in the West for an extended period (more than 30 years). He is now widely recognized as the Father of Yoga in the West. He founded Self-Realization Fellowship(1920) and Yogoda Satsanga Society of India (1917), which continue to carry on his spiritual legacy worldwide."

http://www.yogananda-srf.org/Paramahansa_Yogananda.aspx#.
W3TnbC0ZO1s

The Buddha

"Buddhism started with the Buddha. The word 'Buddha' is a title, which means 'one who is awake' — in the sense of having 'woken up to reality'. The Buddha was born as Siddhartha Gautama in Nepal around 2,500 years ago. He did not claim to be a god or a prophet. He was a human being who became Enlightened, understanding life in the deepest way possible."

https://thebuddhistcentre.com/text/who-was-buddha

Jesus

"Jesus is a religious leader whose life and teachings are recorded in the Bible's New Testament. He is a central figure in Christianity and is emulated as the incarnation of God by many Christians all over the world."

https://www.biography.com/people/jesus-christ-9354382

Other Spiritual Teachers (wise people worth reading)

Dr. Wayne Dyer
Dr. Joe Dispenza
Joseph Campbell
Louise Hay
David R. Hawkins
Dr. Bruce Lipton
Suzi Lula
Dr. Shefali Tsabary
Gregg Braden
Bruce Lipton, Ph.D

Coming soon:
Blessing Mistakes & Mr. Upalupagus's Secret Secrets!

Printed in the United States
by Baker & Taylor Publisher Services